WILD

Discovery CHANNEL

TIME® LIFE BOOKS

DISCOVERY

DISCOVERY COMMUNICATIONS, INC.

John S. Hendricks
*Founder, Chairman, and
Chief Executive Officer*

Judith McHale
President and Chief Operating Officer

Michela English
President, Discovery Enterprises Worldwide

DISCOVERY CHANNEL PUBLISHING

Ann-Marie McGowan
Vice President, Publishing

Rita Thievon Mullin
Editorial Director

Mary Kalamaras
Editor

Marcia Foster
Senior Product Manager

Tracy Fortini
Discovery Channel Retail

Discovery Communications, Inc. produces high-quality television programming, interactive media, books, films, and consumer products. Discovery Networks, a division of Discovery Communications, Inc., operates and manages Discovery Channel, TLC (The Learning Channel), Animal Planet, and Travel Channel. Visit our website at http://www.discovery.com/

TEHABI BOOKS

Nancy Cash, *Managing Editor;* Sarah Morgans, *Editorial Assistant;* Steve Frelingh, *Photo Reseacher;* Jeff Campbell *Copy Proofer;* Ken DellaPenta, *Indexer;* Andy Lewis, *Art Director;* Kevin Giontzeneli, *Assistant Art Director;* Tom Lewis, *Editorial and Design Director;* Sam Lewis, *Webmaster;* Tim Connolly, *Sales and Marketing Manager;* Ross Eberman, *Director of Custom Publishing;* Sharon Lewis, *Controller;* Chris Capen, *President*

Wild Discovery text by Laura Georgakakos and Nancy Cash

Wild Discovery was conceived with and produced by Tehabi Books. "Tehabi"—symbolizing the spirit of teamwork—derives its name from the Hopi Indian tribe of the southwestern United States. As an award-winning book producer, Tehabi works with national and international publishers, corporations, institutions, and non-profit groups to identify, develop, and implement comprehensive publishing programs. Tehabi Books is located in Del Mar, California 92014. www.tehabi.com

Time-Life Books is a division of Time Life Inc.

TIME LIFE INC.

George Artandi: *President and CEO*

TIME-LIFE BOOKS

Stephen R. Frary: *President*

TIME-LIFE CUSTOM PUBLISHING

Terry Newell
Vice President and Publisher

Neil Levin
Vice President of Sales and Marketing

Jennie Halfant
Project Manager

Jennifer Pearce
Director of Acquisitions

Christopher M. Register
Director of Design

Liz Ziehl
Director of Special Markets

Time Life is a trademark of Time Warner Inc. U.S.A.

First printing. Printed in Korea.

Library of Congress Cataloging-in-Publication Data

Wild discovery/ from the editors of
    Discovery Channel Publishing and Time-Life Books
            p.   cm.
    Includes index.
    ISBN 0-7370-0022-8
    1. Zoology. 2. Zoology—Pictorial works.
I. Time-Life Books. II. Discovery Channel Publishing
QL45.2.W55 1998
590—dc21   98-26896
                                                    CIP

Books produced by Time-Life Custom Publishing are available at a special bulk discount for promotional and premium use. Custom adaptations can also be created to meet your specific marketing goals. Call 1-800-323-5255.

Foreword

All of nature moves toward connection and continuity, toward the renewal of life. Within the animal kingdom the eternal cycle of life moves from birth and the ongoing struggle for survival, through courtship and mating, to satisfying the needs for sanctuary and the ties of community, and on, inevitably, toward aging and death.

Genesis is the beginning, birth, the start of a new generation for every species. The urge to live and to reproduce may be the most powerful one in nature, prompting each living creature to seek out its own kind and to renew its species through the creation of a new generation. From pupating insect larvae to hatching crocodile eggs to a zebra foal emerging fully formed and standing upright within minutes of birth, new life appears in an astonishing variety of ways.

An animal's survival in the wild depends upon its ability to secure food and to defend itself. Acting from instinct or observing the behavior of their parents, the young are soon able to hunt, forage, or fish. But in a world where one must eat or be eaten, learning to defend oneself is equally important. Animals must be cunning to avoid becoming prey. The camouflage of coloring and markings also plays a critical role in defense and securing food. In the insect world, a thornbug's shape or a dead-leaf mantid's motionless stance and coloring foil predators and fool prey. Nature's array of armaments is often the decisive factor in the battle for survival.

Connections formed within a species are essential to its continuation. At courtship time, the bizarre and beautiful, the peculiar and bedazzling of the animal kingdom strut their stuff to win the favor of the opposite sex. The urge to procreate, essential to the survival of the species, prompts elaborate courtship rituals aimed at winning a mate—the dance of the red-spotted newt, courtship songs, the bugling of elk, even the painstaking building of the bowerbirds' intricate arbors.

From deep burrows in the undergrowth of the jungle to hideaways in the highest limbs of an African baobab tree, animals find or create sanctuary from predators and pests. The means by which they protect themselves—in termite nests, wolf dens, tortoise shells, and silky webs—comprise a grand display of nature's diversity. Within those refuges, community ties create a network of mutual protection and benefit. From grooming one another against parasites to bringing down larger prey than a single individual could kill alone, group members cooperate to secure a future for their species.

As older animals age and inevitably die, a new generation is born and passes into maturity to mate, seek sanctuary, and form communities of its own. Life is renewed, its circle sustained, as the old gives way to the new.

Genesis

Genesis

There is movement within the nest buried beneath the muddy compost. A chorus of loud barks and cries alerts the female crocodile on guard. Rushing to the nest, she tears through the mud with her claws and jaws. The birth of her offspring has triggered one of the most powerful of urges—fierce maternal protection and care. Her young will surely perish within the hardened mud without her assistance. Reaching her nest, she carefully gathers the unhatched eggs into her jaws, where she rolls them gently between her tongue and palate to help the young escape the leatherlike inner lining of the egg. Once they are freed, she gathers the babies back into her mouth and carries them to the safety of the water's edge, where with jaws opened, she enters the water and gently swishes her head back and forth to release them into the river.

The birth of offspring is the pivotal moment in the life of a member of any species. No other event so strongly signals the parents' arrival into full adulthood. But parental instincts may be triggered even before the birth of young. A dung beetle will bury a ball of dung and then deposit its eggs within the hole, providing its offspring with nourishment upon birth. Even animals that immediately leave their young at birth often take exceptional measures to conceal them from predators and provide them with food. The tarantula hawk wasp lays its eggs in a live but stunned tarantula so its young will have food when they hatch. Butterflies will lay their eggs on a host plant to provide an accessible food source.

Previous spread:

African lion, Tanzania
Anticipating the birth of her cubs, a lioness will leave the safety of the pride and find a secluded spot, where she will give birth to two to four cubs. When the cubs are old enough to follow her, she will introduce them to the pride and their father. Once accepted by the male, they will also enjoy the care and attention of other female lions with litters of their own.

Greater flamingo, Kenya
Flamingos use their bills to mound up mud, small stones, and vegetation to reinforce the nest surrounding their solitary egg. Both parents share nest-tending and brooding responsibilities. At the first signs of hatching, the parents will hold their heads against the egg and make high-pitched contact calls to help the chick imprint with its parents.

Often a single parent takes primary responsibility for young—bear mothers raise their cubs without the involvement of their mates. In other animal families, both parents play a role. Penguin pairs take turns incubating their egg clutches. Sometimes the parenting roles are reversed—a male water bug will carry the female's eggs on its back until they hatch, and male seahorses and sticklebacks manage the birth process.

The process of raising young to maturity may involve several members of a family. A female may be offered assistance at birth by other females of her group. A mother dolphin gives birth to her baby with the help of an experienced "midwife," usually a non-breeding female relative who facilitates the birth and helps to rear the newborn. Closely related female elephants will cross-suckle each other's calves. After a female wolf digs her birthing den early in spring, she and the other wolves of her pack will carry meat to the den and bury it for later use. Following the birth of the pups, pack members will continue to bring food to the den for the female wolf and her young. At only a few months of age, a seal pup will join a nursery group of other babies while its mother goes off in search of food.

Protecting the young is one of the most important tasks of any family group. In the animal world, parents take extraordinary measures to shelter their young from discovery by predators, moving their babies from one nest site to another, ridding their nests of feces that might attract predators, even building physical barriers of sticks, stones, and mud to keep their young out of harm's way. The male oscar, a tropical fish, will carry its young inside its mouth for the first few weeks after birth. A lioness will hide her newborn cubs, changing their location frequently to protect them from hyenas and leopards.

Previous spread:
Nile crocodile, Egypt
Crocodile mothers are very particular about where they dig their nests. The site must have the right thermal characteristics so the eggs will survive.

Brown bear, Alaska
Born the size of a chipmunk, a baby bear is totally dependent upon its mother to protect it and teach it how to survive. Staying with its mother through the first two and one half years of its life, a cub must overcome many obstacles, including starvation, disease, and attack from such predators as wolves, mountain lions, bobcats, eagles—and even adult male bears.

Survival instincts dictate a great deal of animal behavior, but instincts are reinforced with lessons learned by mimicking the behaviors of parents and other members of family groups. After they are weaned, babies must know what to eat. A baby elephant will place its trunk in its mother's mouth to taste what she is chewing. A bear cub will stand alongside its mother as she fishes a river, closely observing her method of catching a salmon. Young chimpanzees carefully mimic their parents' use of tools to smash roots and pry open nuts; they learn to use wadded or chewed leaves as sponges to soak drinking water from recesses in rocks and trees. Soon they master using sticks to collect swarming ants or twisting bent grass stems to fish termites from their mounds. The entire family often helps train the young because the survival of all, the continuation of the species itself, depends upon how well these lessons are learned.

Japanese macaque, Hokkaido, Japan

Providing for her offspring is a long and difficult task for a female Japanese macaque. Food sources can be scarce and infant dependency is lengthy; suckling lasts until the baby is two years old.

Following spread:

Polar bear, Arctic

The Arctic is a terrific training ground for a polar bear cub. Tagging along after its mother, the cub will learn to stalk seals, other small marine mammals, and rodents. Polar bears have even killed reindeer, young walruses, and beluga whales.

American bison, Montana

A bison calf is carefully watched over by its mother and other members of the herd. Both male and female bison will confront an aggressive predator. Lowering their massive horned heads, bison will charge the intruder and try to gore or trample it to death.

Following spread:

White-tailed deer, Virginia

Born in early spring, a white-tailed deer fawn will be cared for by its mother. The male offspring become independent and leave the natal range at approximately 18 months. At the same age, female offspring begin to forage independently but remain near their mothers.

Scaffold web spider, Texas

A scaffold web spider will keep a constant vigil over her egg sac, which is filled with hundreds of soon-to-hatch spiderlings. Upon emerging, they will stay within her web for a few days and then crawl away to build webs of their own.

Three-toed sloth, Costa Rica

Giving birth to a single baby, the female sloth is the sole caregiver. The baby clings to the mother's belly, where it is nurtured for the first six to nine months of life. There it will suckle and be fed foliage from its mother's lips. When the young sloth has matured enough to master the arboreal environment, its mother will depart, leaving it to an independent life among the trees.

Arctic fox, Alaska

Arctic fox parents must survive both savage weather and predation by bears and wolves while trying to rear their litter of pups. Able to reproduce at the early age of 9 or 10 months, paired foxes mate for life and jointly provide their young with small animals and seabirds to eat.

Following spread:
Killer whale, Puget Sound

Killer whales are intelligent and cunning mammals as well as devoted parents. A mother killer whale, or orca, gives birth tail first to an 8-foot-long, 400-pound baby. The baby will stay close by its mother's side until it is about three years old. Even after that, it will remain in her matrilineal family group for life, protected from other orcas in the pod.

Giraffe, Kenya

The connection between a mother giraffe and her baby is established in the days following birth. Licking and nuzzling her baby, the mother is both cleaning it and memorizing its unique smell. She can recognize her young's signature scent among all the others in the herd.

African cheetah, Tanzania

Always on the lookout for danger, a cheetah's keen vision and hearing alert her to both predator and prey. A good teacher, she brings live prey to her four-month-old cubs to give them practice with their hunting skills. When the cubs are a year old, they will begin to accompany her on hunts.

Red-fronted lemur, Madagascar

Red-fronted lemurs are arboreal, as are all lemurs, rarely descending to the ground. The females can be seen scampering together through the trees with their young clinging to their bellies or riding jockey-style on their backs.

Following spread:

African elephant, Namibia

Living in herds made up of adult females, babies, and juveniles of both sexes, female elephants are very attentive mothers. They will nurture and even nurse each other's calves.

Hippopotamus, Zambia

A single hippopotamus young is born on land or in shallow water. Occasionally it is born underwater and must come to the surface for its first breath. When her baby is two weeks old, the mother will introduce it to the herd. Here other females that act as baby-sitters will help to protect it from unfamiliar dominant males who may threaten them.

Pileated woodpecker, Virginia

Feeding its young is a full-time summer job for the adult pileated woodpecker. This species lives in the dense, mature forests of North America. Carpenter ants found in dead trees and old stumps are their major source of food.

Trumpeter swan, Alberta

Trumpeter swans are migratory
waterfowl that return to the
same lake—often the same
nest—year after year to lay
their clutch of eggs. Protective
of the nest site and their
young cygnets, a mated pair of
trumpeters will aggressively
drive other swans from
the lake.

Following spread:

Orangutan, Borneo

An orangutan is an especially
caring mother, nursing and
carrying her baby wherever she
goes. And the relationship
between mother and offspring
is long-lasting; the youngster
remains in her care until it is
about seven years old.

Wolf spider, Texas

With no web to house her egg sac, a female wolf spider carries it on her abdomen. When her spiderlings hatch, they cling to her abdomen or hang from specialized hairs while she forages to feed them. The young enjoy this free ride for several weeks before departing to fend for themselves.

Giant water bug, Mexico

The male giant water bug is sometimes called a toebiter due to the painful nip its piercing and sucking mouth-parts can deliver. It offers an interesting twist on parenting, with the male carrying the female's eggs on its back and caring for the hatched young. Both parents are excellent predators, catching small fish and insects.

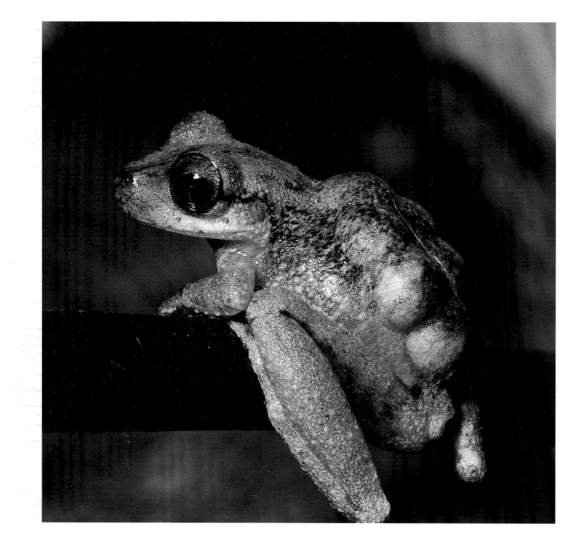

Pygmy marsupial frog, Cloud Forest, Venezuela

Unlike the many frogs that lay their eggs in pools or ponds, the pygmy marsupial frog carries her fertilized eggs in a pouch beneath the skin on her back. When they emerge as tadpoles through a slit in her skin, she slips them into a pool of water where they will develop into frogs.

Capybara, Venezuela

Capybaras, large, water-loving rodents, stay close together in groups while grazing on aquatic vegetation along riverbanks. Whether tending their young, eating, or sunning themselves, they remain alert for the warning clicks, squeaks, and grunts of other capybaras that could announce a cougar or jaguar in the vicinity. Hearing such a call, the entire group will dash into the water for safety.

Following spread:

Mountain goat, Colorado

Craggy cliffs and steep inclines are home to a baby mountain goat, whose cloven hooves and keen balance help it to bound up and down the rocky ledges. Mother goats, called nannies, keep a constant lookout for eagles and hawks that swoop down and snatch up kids from exposed places.

Eat or Be Eaten

Eat or Be Eaten

It has been a long fast since mating, more than 50 days. The king penguin and his mate have spent weeks taking turns incubating their egg. It is time now to eat. Despite his hunger, however, he moves slowly to the water, taking his usual short steps. His bright orange ear patches disappear as he swims out from shore and submerges. With head hunched and feet pressed close to his body to help steer, he looks around for squid, krill, and small fish. Viewed from below, his white underside is nearly indistinguishable from the sunlit surface of the sea. From above, his black back blends in with the dark ocean. Nevertheless, not far from shore, he has been spotted by a creature as dependent upon the sea for food as he is—a leopard seal. Seals move too slowly on land to threaten penguins, but here in the water their danger is so great that any dark spot or shadow causes penguins to send up an alarmed cry and, if possible, get out of the water. But this penguin is unaware of the approach, and the seal is upon him—his teeth sinking into the penguin's chest—before he realizes what is happening. The leopard seal thrashes the penguin repeatedly against the water, but when he momentarily releases his hold to make a grab for the head, the penguin is able to escape toward the ice floe, bloody but alive.

The death dance between hunter and hunted is the most basic and decisive interaction of the natural world. Thus, for most young animals, learning to avoid predators, like

learning to secure food, is among life's most important lessons. Long before their young have developed strength or speed—among the most important skills for both predator and prey— animal parents have begun to teach them how to hunt. A lioness will bring a half-dead animal to her cubs to finish the kill. A striped weasel mother will carry dead mice to her babies in the nest, but as the young mature she will begin to drop injured mice just outside the den and will then coax her young ones into a hunting frame of mind. Those animals without a nurturing parent to guide them rely on instinct—spiders spin webs to trap prey and snakes coil to strike even without having previously observed the behavior.

Nature equips both predator and prey for their particular functions. A woodpecker's hearing is so acute that it can hear a beetle grub chewing wood inside a tree, telling it just where to drill. A lion's tongue is rough enough to scrape meat off bones just by licking them. The short-toed eagle is protected against the venom of its snake prey by thick scales on its legs and thick layers of feathers on its legs and wings. It will even spread its wings just before attacking to encourage the snake to strike it in a safe place. Many prey species are also well-served by protective physical characteristics. The spiny anteater buries itself when predators approach, leaving only its spines visible to pierce a curious snout. The tiny kangaroo rat is equipped with huge eardrums that allow it to hear predators at a distance. The back legs of a cockroach have more than 200 hairs that detect the slightest movement of air. One Texas horned toad puffs itself up when attacked, raising its blood pressure so dramatically that vessels in its eyes burst, shooting blood at an enemy up to 7 feet away.

Camouflage and cunning are critical factors in determining victory or defeat in

Blue shark, Indian Ocean
The blue shark is a solitary hunter that cruises both tropical and temperate waters. It preys primarily upon squid and schooling fish such as sardines, herring, mackerel, and salmon.

an animal's battle for survival. Pattern, color, and number all play a role in the conflict. Squid and octopus can change color to match their surroundings almost instantly to avoid detection by both predator and prey. The disguise of the ant-mimicking spider is so convincing that when wiggling its antennae-like front legs, it can walk among its prey without arousing suspicion. The mesmerizing stripes on a herd of zebras can confuse a predator: where does one animal begin and another end? The same strategy is used by schools of fish, their bars and stripes creating a larger-than-life illusion to confound a marauding predator.

By tooth, fang, or claw, all living creatures secure sustenance and avoid predators, and their success at both determines their species' fate.

Gerenuk, Kenya
Standing on their hind legs, gerenuk gazelles reach into the middle of trees to eat the tender leaves and stems. Their long necks allow them to forage where shorter browsers cannot reach and where the taller giraffes rarely nibble.

Lionfish, Indian Ocean

The venomous lionfish is a formidable prey. Its dorsal spines are lethal weapons used for defense, with poison glands at their base. As predator, the lionfish preys on smaller fish, usually feeding at night.

Prairie falcon, Washington

The prairie falcon is a keen-eyed, swift-flying predator. Agile in its quick aerial maneuvers, it will pluck its prey out of the air or off the ground using its strong taloned feet. Its sharp hooked beak is used to shred the flesh from its victim's body.

Atlantic puffin,

Nova Scotia

An underwater acrobat, the
Atlantic puffin uses its wings as
paddles to maneuver through
the water with exceptional
speed. The puffin can collect
several fish in one dive,
bounding out of the water with
its catch neatly stacked
in its bill.

Following spread:

Hog-nosed viper,

Costa Rica

The venomous hog-nosed viper
nestles among leaf litter
awaiting its prey. The pits at the
sides of its nose are
heat-sensing organs that both
detect warm-blooded animals
and help regulate the amount
of venom injected.

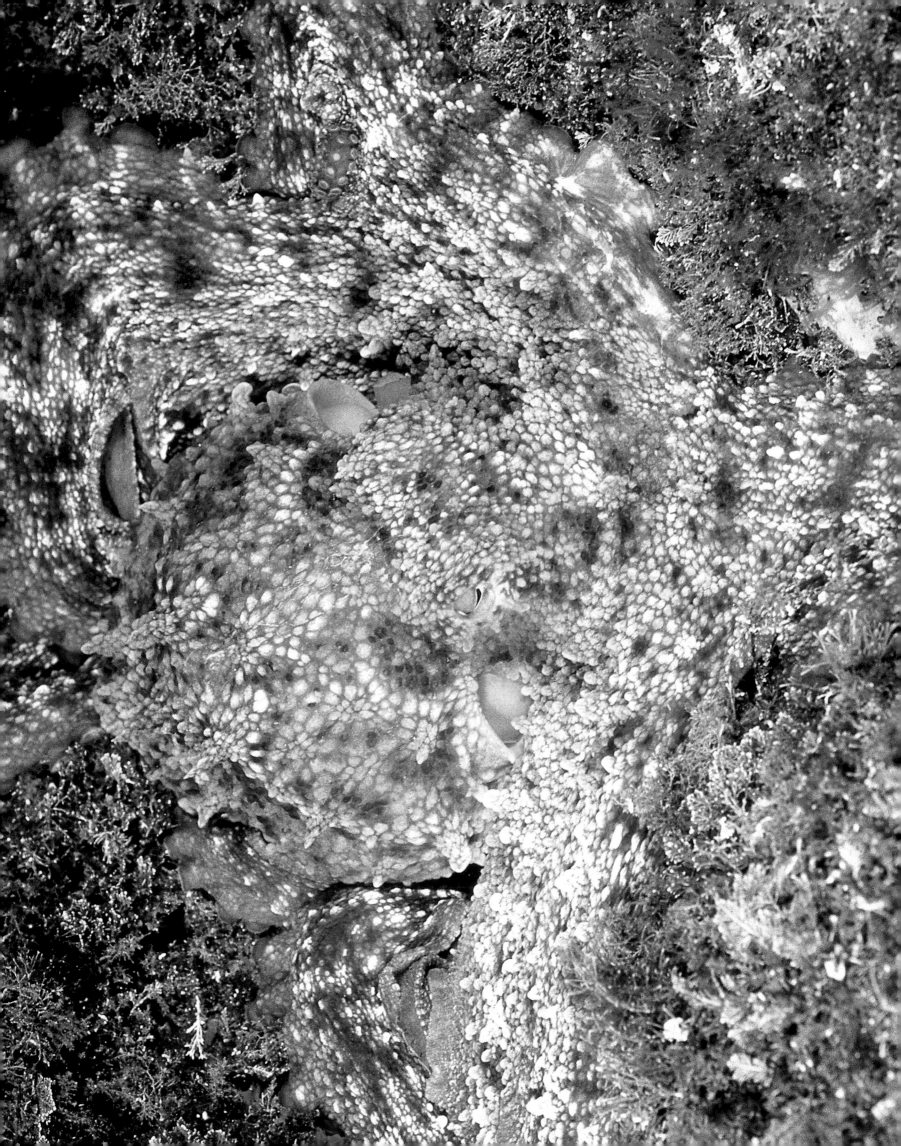

Common octopus, Portugal

When threatened by predators, the octopus changes its normal brown coloring to match its surroundings to conceal itself or protect its eggs. Its colorating can also reflect an octopus's mood—it sometimes turns white when fearful or red when angry.

Henkel's leaf-tailed gecko, Australia

Normally sheltered beneath a rock or log, the Henkel's leaf-tailed gecko sometimes climbs trees to chase after insects. Its mottled skin camouflages it against the textured tree bark, making it less vulnerable to attack when exposed.

Eurasian lynx, Siberia

Even in the snow, the lynx has little trouble overcoming its main prey, the snowshoe hare. It is well suited to the cold-weather environment; its thick fur effectively insulates, and its large feet serve as snowshoes.

Following spread:

African lion, Botswana

Although the female usually hunts more effectively and makes the kill, male lions, though less agile, do hunt. Stalking prey during the late afternoons or at night by moonlight, a lion will select one animal out of a herd and chase it down. Making a quick swipe with its claws to the legs or head of a zebra, the lion takes down its prey. He then bites the throat with his powerful jaws, suffocating the animal.

Chinese mantid, Tennessee

The Chinese mantid can change its coloring to mimic its surroundings. That ability, along with its two large compound eyes, a neck that swivels, and a head that rotates, sets a deadly trap. Snatching its prey with lightning-quick speed, the mantid holds it tightly between hooked, spiked arms. But the mantid itself is prey to bats, frogs, and turtles—even to some other mantids.

Shoebill stork, Uganda

The shoebill, or whale-headed, stork uses its enormous hooked bill to snatch up frogs and fish from the waters of papyrus swamps in central Africa. A solitary bird, it is always on the hunt, wading through the marshlands. But the shoebill can, in an instant, take to the air in graceful flight.

Sunflower sea star,

Baja California

The sunflower sea star has a
very soft body compared to
those of most stars. Its
extraordinary number of arms,
15 to 24, move on hundreds of
tiny suction-cup feet using a
complex hydraulic system that
takes in water through a valve
on the top of its body. An
aggressive hunter, it feeds on
snails, crustaceans, and
anything it can get its arms on,
even its own kind.

Following spread:

Nile crocodile,

Egypt

A crocodile is a relentless
stalker. Swimming just beneath
the surface of the water with
only its eyes and nostrils
exposed, it silently approaches
its unsuspecting prey. With
lightning speed, a crocodile
lunges toward its victim,
grabbing it between powerful
jaws that are lined with razor-
sharp teeth. The struggling
prey is then dragged beneath
the water's surface where the
crocodile violently twists
and thrashes until the
victim drowns.

Six-spotted fishing spider, Florida

This cunning and aggressive spider forms no web but lives and hunts for its prey along stream banks. It submerges itself just under the water's surface to grab a small fish, an unwitting salamander, or an unsuspecting insect. Holding its catch in its jaws, the spider drags it to the surface and consumes it.

Wandering spider, Alabama

Rather than wait for its prey to approach, the wandering spider seeks it out. Like the fishing spider, the wandering spider does not rely on web-spinning. It aggressively stalks its prey through brush and over leaves, uncovering even a camouflaged insect. Pouncing, it dismembers and ingests its prey.

Giant panda, China

The giant panda spends about
12 hours a day eating nearly 35
pounds of bamboo shoots and
leaves. It is threatened partly
due to the increasing scarcity of
bamboo. Except during its brief
courting and mating periods,
covering only a few days
each year, the panda is a
solitary animal.

Following spread:
Bald eagle, Alaska

The bald eagle is a skilled
predator with eyesight so keen
that it can locate prey from a
mile above the ground. Diving
straight down at speeds up to
200 miles per hour, it hits its
prey with incredible force. The
eagle's sharp talons sink into
the prey's body with enough
power to stop its breathing and
crush bones.

Two Together

Two Together

For nearly a year, the two coyotes have played together, slept together, and hunted together across the desert terrain. When the female came into heat, they mated, forging a bond that will last until one of them dies. Now heavy with pups, the female hunts less and must depend upon her mate to provide her food. Together they dig a den site, anticipating the birth of their offspring. The female will not leave the den for weeks once the babies are born. But the bond between the pair is strong, and the male will travel great distances to hunt, returning to the den with his belly full of rodent or carrion and regurgitating it for her and the pups.

Nearly all animal behavior, from fighting to feeding and most everything in between, shares the same ultimate goal—the survival and perpetuation of the species. Courting behaviors initiate the pairing and mating that ensure that goal. Unions between some animals are fleeting and do not extend beyond the coupling, but in other species the bonds between a mated pair, like the coyotes, outlast the rearing of offspring and endure throughout a lifetime. Shared tasks such as nest building and feeding young reinforce these bonds. But the ties that bind are initiated in courtship.

Courtship rituals serve an important function in the animal kingdom. Competition is keen, and males must vie for the favors of the females. The right to mate is earned through sometimes demanding and rigorous courtship displays, which ensure that only the

strongest and healthiest males of a group will pass on their genes to the next generation. Competing male elephant seals wrestle with each other in elaborate matches to win the right to mate. Male African elephants, during what is known as mating pandemonium, or musth, chase and shove and poke one another with their tusks to win mating privileges. Male mountain goats, on the other hand, will lower their backs, take small steps, and keep their horns back in order to appear less threatening and more desirable to the female. Lynx couples spend several days hunting together before mating, which gives the male an opportunity to display his prowess. If a more dominant male appears on the scene, the female will abandon her hunting partner and mate with the newcomer.

Sexual signals are sent by both sexes, but courtship and mating are most often initiated by the male. The bull moose will invite a female to roll in the muddy ditch that he specially prepared for her by urinating in it. Often favored by nature with spectacular coloring, males of many species rely on their dazzling plumage, bright fur, or even pastel-hued scales to attract the more subtly colored females. Dancing and singing, offering gifts or building a cozy abode are employed by males in the animal world to win a mate. All of the male humpback whales in a single ocean sing the same long, complex song at mating time, learning a new melody every year. They sing so loudly that the sound travels underwater for miles.

During courtship, scent, color, and sound announce mating intentions. A female atlas moth's scent can attract a male from 7 miles away. Monarch butterflies rely on scent lingering from the year before to guide them thousands of miles to mating grounds they have never visited before. Annual seasons of rut, scents of musk, and calls of the wild all signal

Previous spread:
Coyote, Montana
Coyotes mate for life with both parents sharing the rearing of their pups. Although largely a nocturnal animal, a coyote will sometimes hunt by day and may travel miles in search of the fruits, grasses, vegetables, and small mammals that comprise its diet.

Red-spotted newt, New Hampshire
Like many of the salamanders and newts, the red-spotted newt is energetic in its courting. Late in the evening, following the first warm rains of the season, male newts begin their march. Gathering together at breeding ponds, they begin to dance, wiggling and writhing their bodies back and forth all through the night. By early morning, the water's surface is sprinkled with their white spermatophores—capsules containing spermatozoa—ready to be picked up by the females.

urges to perpetuate the species. While some courtship displays are more elaborate than others, all are distinctive and effective. To woo its female, the male Emperor of Germany bird of paradise hangs upside down, his exquisite plumage creating an exotic, cascading feather exhibit. A male gorilla will strut and beat his chest. And then there are the truly spectacular and intricately choreographed displays, such as the dance of the ostrich. The female ostrich, anxious to mate, makes the first amorous overture, and the male, aroused by her scent, begins his seductive dance. Together they move to a symbolic nest site, chosen by the male, where the dance continues until the two finally mate.

Courtship is not always a scene of dancing and tenderness. It can be a bloody business. Courting postures are often only slightly modified threat postures. The male caribou's behaviors of antagonism and courtship are so similar that females will often flee when he would most like them to stay. The courtship displays of the walrus can initiate violent fighting among the bulls. Battles may erupt among black rhinos during mating as well, but the opponents are the male and female, who may seriously gore each other with their horns. After mating, the wounded pair go their separate ways. But whether blood-caked or soothed by song, courtship accomplishes its vital objective: the continuation of the species.

Guanaco, Argentina

Guanacos mate and raise their young on the windy Patagonian plains in Argentina. These humpless camels resemble llamas without wool. Their family groups include a single breeding male and several females with their offspring.

Market Squid, California

In the shallow coastal regions of the Pacific, thousands of squid begin their mating behavior. To attract the favor of a female, a male will perform a complex array of movements and courtship displays, including coloration changes. He wraps himself around a willing female and deposits his sperm. Later, during the night, the female deposits fertilized eggs by the hundreds in transparent and sticky gelatinous capsules that she attaches to solid objects on the ocean floor. After egg laying, she departs, leaving the young to hatch alone 30 days later.

Siberian tiger, China

Normally a solitary animal, a young, male Siberian tiger may cross over into another male's territory and challenge him for mating privileges with females. Although a tiger will not mate with a single female for life, he will mate with selected females for a number of seasons.

Red-eyed tree frog, Costa Rica

Red-eyed tree frogs engage in acrobatic mating performances. Competition for females is often a test of endurance. Males will battle each other intensely while locked in a tight embrace. Special adhesive toe pads help to attach them securely to the surface of tree limbs or leaves during the match. After the male mates with a female, the female uses her toe pads to secure herself to limbs in order to attach the eggs to the undersides of leaves overhanging pools of water. When the tadpoles emerge, they drop into the water, where they continue their development into frogs.

Black-browed albatross, Falkland Islands

The albatross is one of the largest of all flying birds. It spends its life at sea, returning to land only to breed. Sleeping on the water or even while gliding in the air, the albatross feeds on fish it snatches from just beneath the water's surface.

Grunion, California

The mating phenomenon of the grunion is one of the most intriguing in nature. The small silvery fish come on shore to spawn in the wet sand for a few nights following the full moons between March and June. Females ride the waves in to shore at high tide, and if they find no males waiting, they catch the next wave out and then try again. When they do find males, the females swim as far up onto the beach as possible, then arch their bodies and wriggle their tails back and forth, literally drilling their bodies into the sand. Males curve their bodies around the females, depositing their milt as the females lay thousands of eggs in the sand. They then wriggle themselves free and ride the next wave out to sea.

Great gray bowerbird, Australia

The male great gray bowerbird builds and decorates a courting structure to entice its mate. The bower of sticks may be constructed with a moss floor and woven vine roof. He may even decorate the bower with snail shells or brightly colored fruits. Bowerbirds court and mate in the bower, but the females raise their young alone in nearby cup-shaped nests built without the males' help.

Following spread:
Stick-mimicking grasshopper, Ecuador

Only the smaller male could distinguish this female stick-mimicking grasshopper from the stick it stands upon. Their camouflage protects them from their natural predators, birds, small animals, and other insects, allowing them to successfully court and mate.

Blue Peafowl, India

Few birds offer a more spectacular courtship display than the peacock spreading and vibrating its glorious blue-spotted tail. It lifts the long, iridescent plumes of its feathered train high in the air and then shivers violently, causing the stiff quills to rattle. Strutting in full display, it emits a loud scream that announces its intentions to the female.

Giraffe, Kenya

Male giraffes must work their way to the top of a herd's ranking order before they may mate with females. Giraffes are generally peaceful animals, and the males' battles follow strict protocol. Neck postures and bowing displays send messages of dominance. Once initiated, confrontations can escalate to neck slapping that can be heard 50 yards away. Nevertheless, other than occasional jabs to the neck or flank by a foe's horns, serious harm is rarely caused by these battles.

Black rhinoceros, Tanzania

Usually a solitary animal, the black rhinoceros male becomes very friendly to the female in courtship. He will nuzzle her along her sides and shoulders, and nudge her with his horn and head in mock sparring behavior. This heavily armored Romeo will even rest his chin on her rump during his coy courting maneuvers. But mating itself can become violent, and either animal can be seriously wounded by horn jabs.

Gray angelfish, Bahamas

Courting gray angelfish are very shy, but will aggressively defend their territory. Like several varieties of angelfish, gray angelfish change color. They are black with yellow stripes as juveniles and turn gray as they mature.

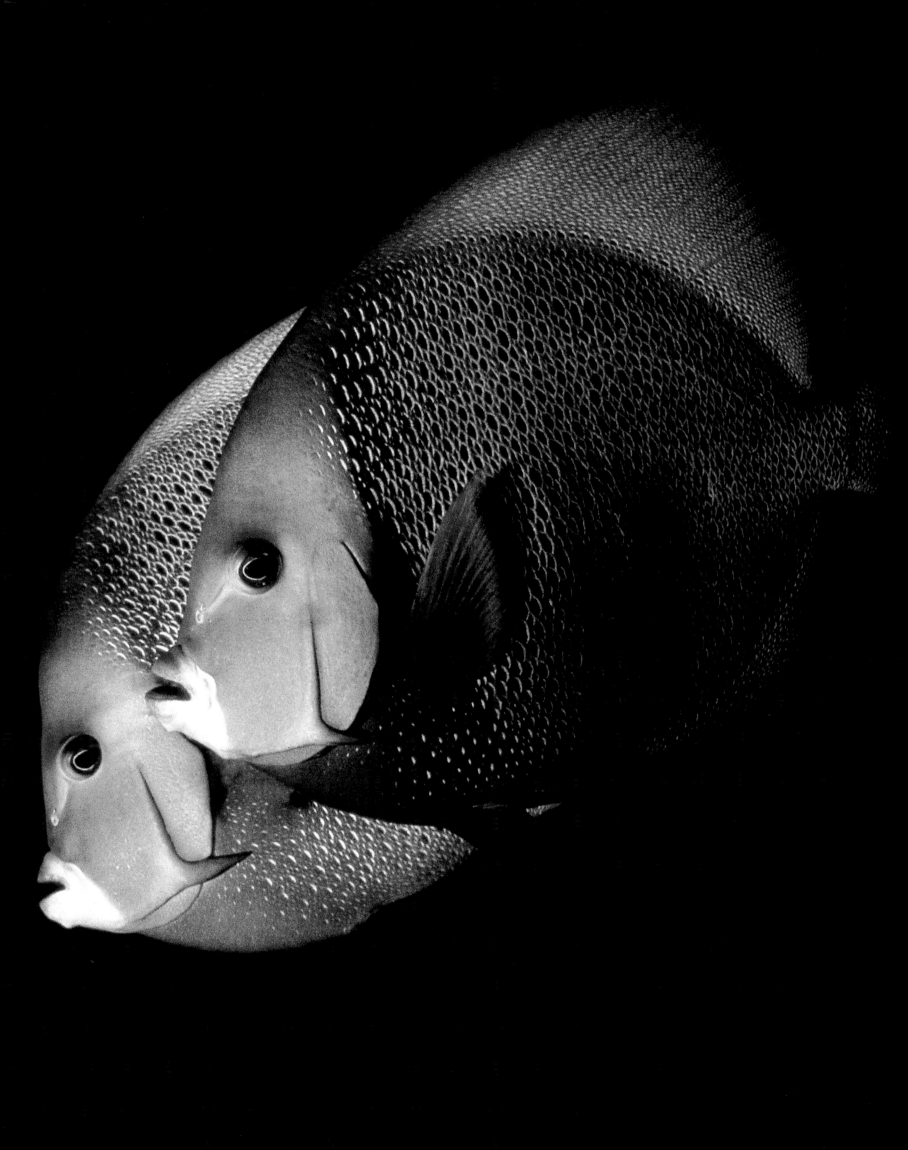

Previous spread:

Plain's zebra, Tanzania

A battle over females between the dominant zebra male and a younger male challenger can be a real kicking and biting match. The older, established stallion will strongly guard his harem and fend off suitors. A young mare in her first breeding season will exhibit her willingness to mate with outside males. But the dominant stallion of her harem, usually her father, will groom and coax her into mating with him. Older, seasoned females extend an invitation stance to their stallion.

African elephant, Kenya

When a male African elephant comes into musth—a heightened sexual rutting condition caused by hormonal changes—he becomes unpredictable and touchy. He will engage in fights with other males and will even attack inanimate objects. Males that are more dominant will avoid him, but females will seek him out.

Previous spread:

Parson's chameleon,

Madagascar

Parson's chameleon are aggressive lovers. In brilliant full color and set for battle, the love game begins. Struggles between males vying for both territory and females usually result in one of the males backing down. But the treetop courtship between a male and female can be equally violent; biting and scratching, the pair sometimes falls to the ground.

Red deer, England

With the scent of estrus in the autumn air, the red deer stag, called an elk in the United States, gathers his harem of females. In rut, the stag will bugle his dominance, warning other males in the area to stay away. Bugling can be heard throughout the rutting season.

Following spread:

Bengal tiger, India

Curling the lip in a gaping facial grimace is known as the flehmen response. Using a specialized sensory organ located above its palate, the Bengal tiger can detect the scent of an estrous female. The usually solitary cat will then seek out her company and, after a brief courting, mate with her.

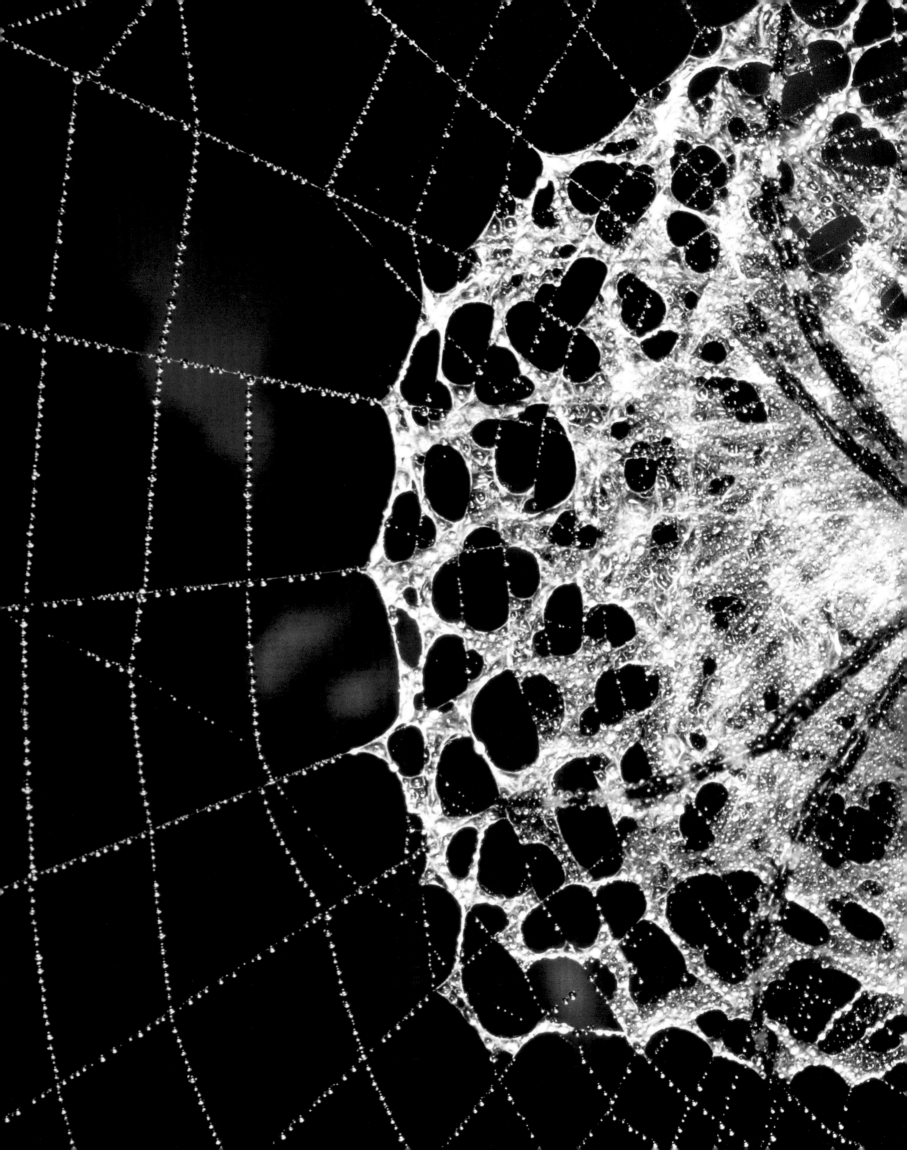

Sanctuary

Sanctuary

The new lodge is nearly finished. The beaver parents and their young work furiously to "winterize" their dome-shaped dwelling in the middle of the pond, where they will spend the long months until springtime's thaw. Inside and underwater, they have cached a winter's food supply—twigs and branches of deciduous trees cut down with their extremely sharp teeth. The nearby dam, cemented with mud and leaves, impounds enough water to surround the lodge so that both entrances are underwater—a reliable security system against predators. One entrance was used to carry in their winter food supply, and the other will be their own private access to the lodge. As long as their pond does not freeze over completely, they will be free to come and go. With a final scattering of wood shavings to line the lodge, it is complete—a fine, snug sanctuary.

Sanctuary is home: a nest high in a tree, an underground burrow, a chamber inside a rotting log, or even under the water's surface. Sanctuaries may be one-time refuges from a hot sun or a chilly night, or they may be retreats used repeatedly. Some are places to which animals return again and again, familiar spots where they can rest after foraging or hunting. Bears return to hibernate in the same den year after year. Leopards will keep returning to the same tree to sleep in its branches, marking it as their own by clawing it. Tent bats will return daily to nest on the same leaf for up to seven weeks. Eagles return to the same nest, enlarging it during each breeding season. One nest in Iowa was used for 40 years by pairs of

Previous spread:

Silver argiope spider, Panama

A web is more than just sanctuary to a spider. It may serve as nursery for its young, cradling them until they emerge from their egg sac cocoon. But for the argiope, a web is carefully crafted primarily to ensnare prey. Some spiders' webs are even large and strong enough to capture birds. Others used as nets are thrown over prey that venture too close.

Elf owl, Arizona

A hole in a saguaro, a sycamore tree, or even a telephone pole is home to the smallest owl in the world. Laying a clutch of two to five eggs, the tiny elf owl, the size of a sparrow, feeds its young mostly on insects while enjoying a more varied diet itself. Strictly nocturnal, it sees quite well to hunt in the dark. The elf owl's large, yellow eyes seek out centipedes, scorpions, and even the occasional small bird or lizard.

eagles — it weighed 4,000 pounds when it finally crashed to the ground.

Throughout the animal kingdom, sanctuaries vary widely in size, type, and location. The elaborate set of chambers created by leafcutter ants may extend 49 feet across, while the nests of tiny bee hummingbirds are less than 2 inches across. Prairie dogs, working together, construct elaborate, miles-long tunnels underground. Birds and chimpanzees nest in trees, while nearby caterpillars curl and tether their silk around a single leaf to create a cozy abode. While tall grasses may provide safe haven to a solitary cheetah, a nearby termite mound teems with up to two million insects. Among birds, the most elaborately and intricately constructed of all nests are those of the weavers. Using grasses and strips of leaves, the weavers create round or basketlike pouches with entrances located at the bottom and nest chambers on top. Social weavers of Africa interweave their nests with neighboring ones, forming a huge communal structure.

The quest for sanctuary may even involve more than one species. A cool, muddy bog can be home to both warthog and bullfrog. Wasps and bees have been known to renovate an abandoned mouse burrow. A remora attaches itself securely to the side of a swift-moving shark, while the spine-cheek anemonefish hides among venomous sea anemones, unthreatened by their stings.

The most important function of sanctuary is protection, particularly of the young or newly born. Grebes build floating nests to protect their young from land predators. The queen of a leafcutter ant colony will spend several months completely sealed off in her chamber to lay her eggs in safety. A male hornbill will likewise use mud to seal his mate and

Beaver, Idaho
Beavers continually forage for food and building materials to construct or repair their homes. Using oversized front teeth, a beaver chews and gnaws through the bark and soft cambium layers of trees and limbs. It will eat some of the tender twigs on the spot and will carry other small branches and wood chips back to the lodge to be stored as winter food.

their eggs into their tree-trunk nest, feeding her through a tiny opening. After the eggs hatch, the mother pecks her way out of the nest, and the young then replaster the hole, walling themselves in again until they are ready to fly. When adult mongooses go out for the day to hunt, they leave their young behind in the safety of their burrow. But the adults also have daytime refuges and boltholes scattered across their extensive territories to which they can escape from danger or simply retire for a nap. Tortoises have a far easier arrangement. They only have to pull in head, tail, and legs to avail themselves of all that is offered by their mobile sanctuary—seclusion, protection, home.

White tent bat, Honduras

Tiny white tent bats find a *heliconia* leaf the perfect sanctuary in which to sleep away the day. They chew away both ends of the midrib of the leaf until it folds over and creates a snug hollow within. The tent bats then climb into the hollow and snuggle together, holding on to the leaf's midrib with their back feet.

Following spread:

Cleaning shrimp, Celebes Sea

Cleaning shrimp live in a symbiotic relationship with much of the marine life of the coral reef. They groom many of their hosts by eating the parasites off their bodies. Whether seeking refuge among the tentacles of venomous anemones, finding sanctuary in the nooks and crevices of mushroom coral, or living on the bodies of certain jellyfish, the cleaning shrimp's unique behavior allows it to enjoy both a bounty of food and protection from predators.

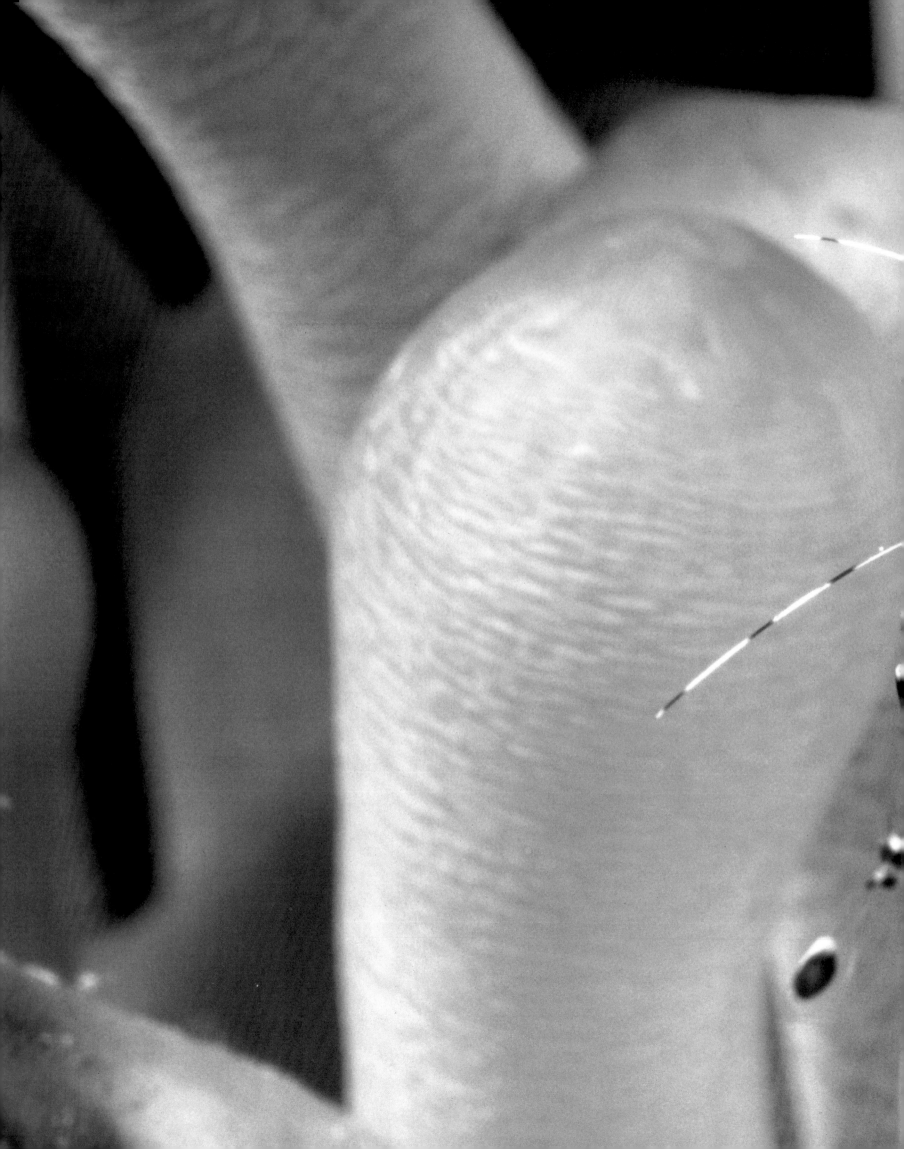

Canada goose, Manitoba

The cooperation between a mated pair of Canada geese is one reason for the species' success at rearing young. Working together to build a nest of grasses and sticks to shelter their clutch of eggs, the adults guard their just-hatched goslings until late summer, when the young will be old enough to fend for themselves.

Thornbug, California

The thornbug is almost a perfect mimic. Virtually indistinguishable from the thorn on the rose bush, it lives undetected by most predators. Not only do its shape and coloration fool predators, but its habit of walking upside down on the rose bush stem and remaining immobile at the slightest movement of the stem contribute to its charade.

Leaf-mimic katydid, Costa Rica

The leaves of trees and shrubs are perfect hiding places for the leaf-mimic katydid. Its unique coloring and shape provide sanctuary amid trees and shrubs where it feeds on foliage. And the epidermal layers of the leaves serve as a nursery for the katydid's eggs.

Following spread:
Dead-leaf mantid, Malaysia

A dead-leaf mantid finds protection among the leaf litter on the forest floor. The mantid's cryptic disguise and coloration give this fierce predator a tactical advantage over its unsuspecting prey and shield it from detection by its own enemies.

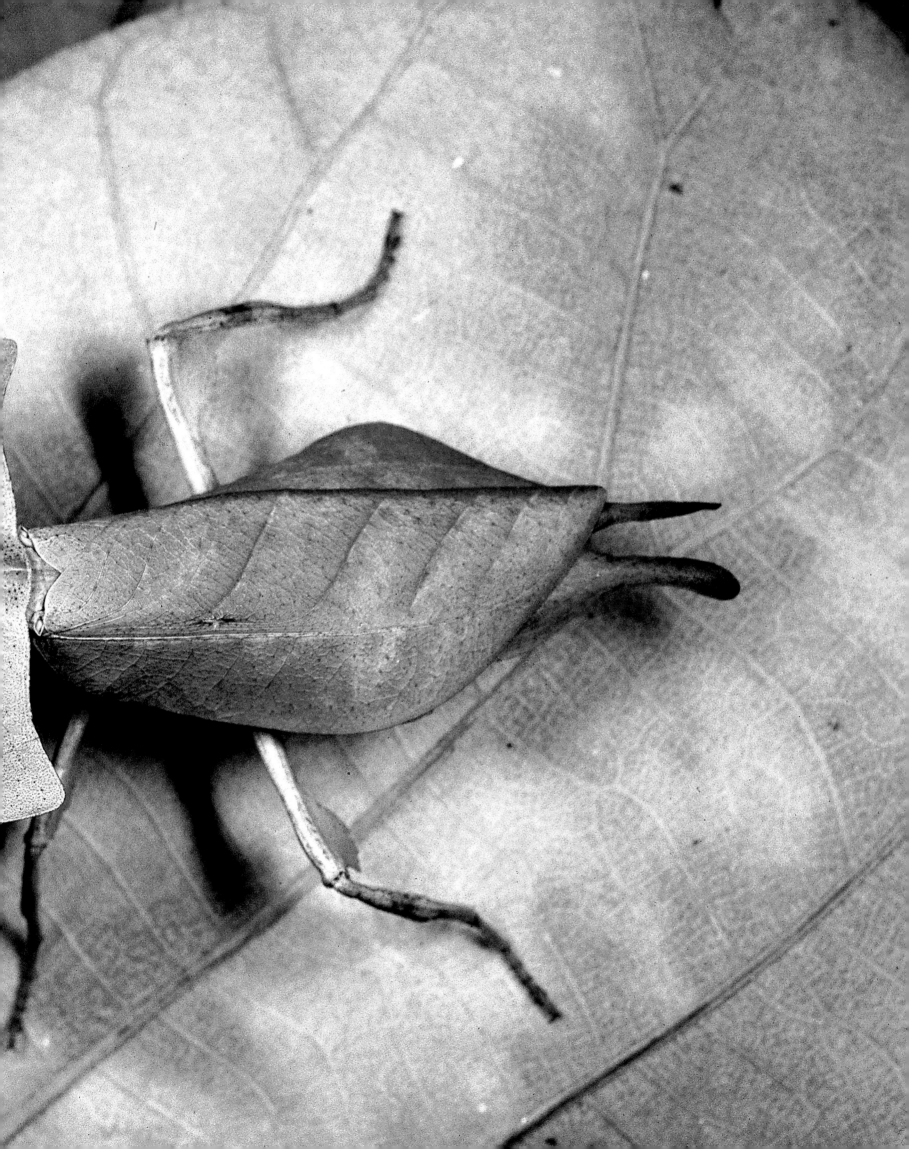

Antarctic blue-eyed cormorant, Antarctica

By nesting high on isolated rock surfaces, the Antarctic blue-eyed cormorant protects itself from potential predators, such as leopard seals.

Florida manatee, Florida

The gentle manatee, once mistaken by sailors for the mythical mermaid, is at home in the shallows of slow-moving rivers, estuaries, and the warm saltwater bays of coastal regions. This nonaggressive herbivore spends most of its day eating aquatic plants while swimming close to the surface. Because of the camouflage patterns created on its skin from the filtered light above, it often passes undetected.

Hairy hermit crab, Galápagos Islands

Like most hermit crabs, the hairy hermit crab prefers a snug home. This crustacean uses empty gastropod shells as protective cover for its soft abdomen. As it outgrows its shell, it carefully selects a larger one, tryng it on for size, weight, and even color contrast. Without the protection of its shell, the hermit crab is a tasty morsel just waiting to be snatched up.

Barn owl, Wisconsin

Barn owls do not construct nests, but instead they seek sanctuary in abandoned buildings, holes in trees, and crevices. They remain with the same mate for several years and return to use the same nesting site season after season.

Argentine horned frog, Uruguay

The mottled coloring of this horned frog makes for a very deceptive disguise when it sits in an algae pond. Its perfect camouflage makes it an unpleasant surprise to any unsuspecting mouse, salamander, or fish that happens to come within its reach. All are eaten whole by this voracious horned frog.

Silky pygmy anteater, Trinidad, West Indies

The silky pygmy anteater, the smallest known anteater, lives high in a ceiba tree. Its soft, yellow fur perfectly matches the color and sheen of the tree's seedpods, concealing it from the harpy eagles, eagle hawks, and spectacled owls that prey upon it. The anteater's tree house supplies both shelter and a steady supply of food—ants, termites, and beetles.

Red fox, England

A litter of red fox kits is tucked away in a den beneath a fallen tree. The mother, away hunting, has hidden her pups well. Their tawny coloring blends in with their surroundings, protecting them from predators.

Following spread:

Mule deer, Montana

Nestled down in the meadow grass, a mule deer fawn waits for the return of its mother. Sheltered from view, the fawn will remain motionless. Its coloring and spotted coat help to protect it. If the fawn is threatened, its mother, if she is near, will put herself at risk to draw off the predator.

Nudibranch,

California

Elegant in color and form, nudibranchs are found in areas as far south as coral reefs of warm tropical waters and as far north as the cold waters off Alaska. Many nudibranchs are able to camouflage themselves to resemble their backgrounds. Over time, some have even taken on the coloring of their host plant or animal. Lacking shells for defense, the nudibranch swims well and possesses skin glands that secrete sulphuric acid.

Following spread:

Leopard, Kenya

The leopard finds a branch high in a tree a suitable retreat. Like most cats, leopards have no difficulty climbing trees. A lofty perch provides a lookout site and a cool spot for a nap. Leopards will drag their kill up into a tree to secure it from theft, to eat it in peace, or to store it for a later meal.

Community

Community

As the morning sun reaches the entrance to its underground burrow, the first meerkat up for the day makes his way outside and begins his watch. Standing up on his tiny hind legs, his thin tail pointing straight down to the ground, he assesses his surroundings, searching out any potential danger with a sweeping gaze. Seeing no predators in the area, he gives the "all-clear" call. It is only then that the rest of his colony ventures out from the burrow to join him. Standing guard to keep watch for danger is an important responsibility in meerkat society, one that continues throughout the day as other members of the group take their turn on sentry duty, alerting all to any threat.

Social interactions are necessary for the survival of any animal group. From the simplest community of a single male and female and their offspring to the more complex society of several adults together with their young, members communicate with one another and coexist cooperatively in ways that benefit the group. The most elaborate working societies may be those of bees, termites, and ants, which work within a complex social caste system. Food gathering, guard duty, and even mating privileges are relegated and designated by rank. A school of fish or pride of lions operates communally with a well-orchestrated division of labor and social hierarchy; within these societies, child-rearing responsibilities and food gathering for weak or younger members are shared. Together the group accomplishes what no single

Previous spread:
Spine-cheek anemonefish, Papua New Guinea
In a unique relationship, anemonefish seek protection from their fish predators by hiding within the venomous tentacles of the sea anemone. Mucus coating their bodies protects them from the anemone's stinging cells. In return for its hospitality, the anemone is protected from its own predators by these fiercely territorial fish.

Meerkat, Botswana
Meerkats are highly social animals that live in tight-knit groups of up to 30 members— a dominant female with her mate and successive litters of their offspring. Group members recognize each other by sight and smell and are suspicious of newcomers and intruders.

member could. Armies of tiny margined burying beetles can drag a mouse or bird carcass as far as 15 feet. Hooking their bodies together, ants form long, living bridges to permit hunting parties to ford bodies of water.

Food is certainly more easily obtained by individuals working together. During cooperative fishing sessions, some dolphin and whale species collectively herd schools of fish to the water's surface, where the fish are devoured. Although more mouths will share in the spoils, hunting or foraging can be done more frequently and larger prey can be sought by a group than by individuals working alone. Hyenas and wolves routinely surround and kill prey larger than themselves. Piranhas travel in teams, and once the "scout" piranha seizes a victim, the flow of blood alerts the rest of the team that a meal is ready to be shared.

Community life benefits prey as well as predator. White-tailed deer silently warn one another of nearby danger with a flash of the undersides of their tails. Baboons and musk-oxen protect themselves by assembling into group formations. The group may be more visible to predators than an individual would be, but the group is more formidable, and single members become less vulnerable to attack. A hungry grouper's advance upon a tiny fish is thwarted by the illusion of a much larger fish created by many small fish swimming in formation. There is truly safety in numbers, and by cooperating, group members even reduce some of the risks inherent to group life itself. Grooming each other, called allogrooming, diminishes the danger of disease posed by parasites and binds members together through links of indebtedness—if you groom me today, I am more likely to be here to reciprocate tomorrow.

Monarch butterfly, California

Every year migrating monarch butterflies fly thousands of miles to traditional nesting places. Some fly to wintering sites at high elevations where they cluster in trees up to four months to wait out winter's freezing temperatures. Millions hibernate together to conserve energy before continuing their journey in the spring. The monarch is the only insect on earth that migrates annually over continental distances. It is estimated that 300 million monarch butterflies migrate to Mexico every year. Others migrate to California coastal sites.

Community ties provide protection and comfort. An intense and enduring tie links an elephant mother and calf. A nine-year-old elephant will continue to spend half its time within five yards of its mother. Elephant mothers and daughters may remain together in matriarchal family herds for as long as 50 years. In mole-rat colonies and gazelle herds, female members share the group's mothering duties.

Even members of different species can live together in mutually beneficial relationships and communities. Egyptian plovers clean the teeth of crocodiles. Lizards and snakes share termite mounds to incubate their eggs. Badgers and coyotes sometimes hunt together. A tortoise burrow may house raccoons, rabbits, lizards, and rats. Whether joined together for a lifetime or a single season, social animals rely on one another for a range of support. Links between group members can be strengthened through such reinforcing behaviors as the howling of wolves and the chorus of hyenas. Even animals that do not normally travel in groups, such as tigers or leopards, will briefly share community life at mating time. The bonds of community form a web of increased safety, increased access to food, and the shared knowledge that enhances a group's ability to survive and, indeed, to thrive.

Leafcutter ant, Brazil

Leafcutter ants live in colonies of up to one million. They carry leaves back to their gardens to propagate a specific kind of fungus that they eat.
This fungus-eating ant lives in a sophisticated society of regulated castes: soldiers, three classes of workers, the reproductive males, and the egg-laying queen. The soldiers protect the colony and each of the three worker castes has one specific duty—cleaning the nest, searching for leaves of woody plants, and transporting pieces of leaves to the colony. Each caste member performs its specific duty to ensure the health and continuation of the ant colony.

Indiana bat, Missouri

The Indiana bat dwells along the streams and rivers of northern Missouri. Colonies hibernate in cool caves and emerge in early spring to migrate to summer roosting and foraging areas. Males and females separate in summer, when 50 to 100 females will gather together in maternity colonies to give birth. The young are raised beneath the loose bark of living and dead trees. Some of the males migrate to the floodplains and upland forests, while others remain near their hibernation cave to which the females will return at summer's end.

Greater and lesser flamingo, Africa

Entire populations of flamingos take to the skies seemingly on impulse, but almost certainly in order to find better foraging or nesting areas. They may fly long distances to ponds full of alkaline water and food. They congregate in huge colonies—numbers as high as two million have been reported.

King penguin,

Sub-Antarctic

Penguins are among the most
social of birds. They form
huge nesting colonies, some
numbering in the millions. King
penguins raise their young in
the same rookeries where they
were raised, on beaches and in
areas free of snow and ice that
are accessible to the sea.

Following spread:

Plain's zebra,

South Africa

Zebras will congregate in large
herds at watering sites and in
good grazing areas. But they
live in smaller groups of a single
stallion and several mares
with their foals. Communal
grooming and touching help
maintain close relationships
within this family unit. Members
recognize one another by sight,
smell, and sound.

Previous spread:

Tundra swan, Alaska

Tundra, or whistling, swans migrate in great flocks to summer nesting sites in the Arctic regions of northern Alaska and Canada. Congregating on waterways, they feed and raise their young. In the fall, they leave for the warmer climates of the east and west coasts of the United States. The flocks can be heard making a high-pitched, whistling sound as they fly high overhead in straight lines.

Sergeant major, Indo-Pacific Ocean

Schools of brightly colored sergeant majors roil near the surface to feed. Sergeant majors, or bengals as they are sometimes called, have a reputation as bold defenders of their territory. Males guarding a patch of eggs are vigorous in their vigilance, even nipping at intruders. The barred coloring of a feeding school create a spectacular effect.

Ladybird beetle, California

Ladybird beetles, or ladybugs as they are known in the United States, fly to overwintering sites in the autumn. As many as 80,000 of the beetles may congregate at the base of trees, or under logs and rocks.

Musk-ox, Alaska

When threatened by Arctic wolves, their natural enemy, musk-oxen immediately run together to form a tight circle. The adults face out toward the predators while the calves remain hidden and protected within the circle. Unless the herd stampedes, this defensive circle is impenetrable. If only one predator threatens, the musk-oxen will stand shoulder to shoulder, forming a solid line, and a single musk-ox may even charge the would-be attacker.

Following spread:

Sea nettle jellyfish, Pacific Ocean

The sea nettle jellyfish packs a walloping sting. Despite its name, it is not actually a fish at all but rather a relative of the sea anemone and coral. Jellyfish propel themselves with a pumping or pulsating movement of their round, umbrella-like bodies. They may move singly or in large groups that can travel many miles in a single day.

African lion, Kenya

A pride is made up of lionesses
that are mothers and daughters
or aunts of the same family line.
Lionesses within a pride groom
each other, cooperatively hunt,
and nurture each other's young.

Moray eel, Celebes Sea

The moray eel and the cleaner
wrasse maintain a mutually
beneficial relationship. The
normally aggressive eel will
quickly snap up any prey within
its reach, its razor-sharp teeth
and powerful jaws inflicting a
deadly bite. But it makes an
exception for the cleaner
wrasse, a tiny fish that rids the
eel of parasites on its mouth,
gills, and body.

Emperor penguin, Antarctica

The emperor is the largest of the penguins, standing almost 44 inches tall. Walking together in groups or congregating in colonies of thousands along the shoreline, these large birds rely on one another for protection, food, and child-rearing.

Following spread:

Walrus, Bering Sea

Walruses are gregarious animals that live in same-sex herds. During the breeding season, the bulls become aggressive and territorial, defending not only their dominance and the right to their harem but also their spot on the beach. The tusks on a bull can grow to be 3 feet long. They are used for fighting off rivals and are a status symbol in the herd.

**Schooling bannerfish,
French Polynesia**

Startling in color, schooling
bannerfish swim together in
tight groups. As the school
moves as one, their bars create
a mesmerizing pattern.
Swimming *en masse* protects
individual fish from predation.

Bighorn sheep, Colorado

Bighorn sheep most commonly gather in herds of eight to ten. They graze intermittently throughout the day on grasses and sedges in alpine meadows and on mountain slopes. During rutting season, the males battle over mating rights to a particular female. They run at each other, reaching speeds as fast as 20 miles per hour, and crash their great horned heads together. A battle can last more than 24 hours until one of the combatants gives in, and the sound of their collisions can be heard at great distances.

Following spread:

Eastern white pelican, Kenya

Eastern white pelicans are rather shy birds that nest in communal breeding grounds hidden in island coves. Weighing as much as 25 pounds, they often spar with other pelicans over nesting sites. They are protected from injury by special horny plates that develop on their bills during breeding season. To feed, flocks of pelicans fly in unison, then plunge headfirst, one after another, into the water for fish.

African cheetah, Tanzania

The female cheetah is a solitary animal until her cubs are born, and then she stays with them for at least a year. As the sole provider for her family, the mother cheetah works hard to care for her cubs, making kills almost daily to keep them and herself fed. As the cubs mature, they begin to help with the hunts until they are ready to fend for themselves.

Following spread:
Wildebeest, Kenya

Wildebeest herds are enormously large—yearly migrations involve as many as one million animals all moving at once. The herd keeps its steady pace for weeks until it reaches its designated grazing regions. From birth, wildebeests have remarkable stamina. Calves can stand and run within three to seven minutes after birth.

Circle of Life

Circle of Life

Since leaving the sea, the sockeye salmon's journey has been long and brutal. Swimming up the mouth of the river was easy, but now, jumping up the falls is taking its toll. Its body is bruised from continual bludgeoning against the rocks, and pieces of its flesh have been torn away by the thundering flood of water from the overhead spillway. The salmon's urge to move upstream, however, to return to the site of its birth to spawn, is too great to stop. Nothing save sheer exhaustion or a predator's attack will divert it from its course. Once past the falls, the salmon pushes on. Hormonal changes are turning its skin a deep red, and its snout is now enlarged and curved into a hook in anticipation of the mating run. With its bottom fins worn away and its flesh hanging in shreds, it finally reaches the stream of its birth. There it finds itself surrounded by others—males ready to fight and females already heavy with eggs. As his chosen female busily digs a nest in the streambed, he engages with another male in a fight over her. Once he has driven off his opponent, with a last burst of energy, the male salmon releases his sperm over the eggs that are already deposited in the gravel. Only then, with his body battered and his life spent, does he die.

Time passes inevitably and the processes of aging bring a slowing, a diminishment. Many of the biological systems of an animal are affected in the last third of its life. Metabolic and hormonal changes, deterioration of various organs and teeth, and partial or total loss of the senses all render the aging animal more vulnerable to a predator's attack.

Previous spread:

Sockeye salmon, Alaska

Driven by the innate urge to spawn, sockeye salmon journey from the ocean to the very stream where they were born. Just before dying they give life to their offspring with the laying and fertilizing of their eggs, completing their journey.

Western lowland gorilla, Uganda

Few animals in the wild live to be old. Most are attacked by predators or die of injury or disease. Gorillas can live up to 25 years in the wild and a troop leader that has survived poaching by humans or other threats for 15 to 20 years, will begin to develop the characteristic sheen of the silverback. But at that age he may no longer be able to withstand challenges from younger, stronger males. Eventually he will lose his position as leader, spending his days resting and foraging,

**Sockeye salmon eggs
and hatchlings,
British Columbia**

One to two years following their
hatching, these sockeye
salmon fry will feel the same
irresistable urge their parents
felt to journey from the stream
where they were born back to
the sea. Two years later,
they will return to
the stream to spawn.

Sockeye salmon, Alaska

The spawning migration from
saltwater to the hatching site is
a rigorous one for the salmon.
There are predators to be
avoided and falls to be
negotiated. Only the fat and
strong will make it. A sockeye
salmon may jump again and
again at a falls until exhaustion,
success, or a waiting bear ends
its struggle.

A gradual loss of muscle mass and tone diminishes an individual's speed and strength, potentially threatening the entire herd or group. The old, like the young, are the easiest prey.

Relations between older and younger group members may change or cease altogether. In the same way that a tree will begin to hold back key minerals from a dying leaf, some animal groups will ease an aging member out, conserving resources for younger members of reproductive age. As a result, these members may form a new group of their own. Older male seals, along with any other seals not involved in breeding, form separate herds near the breeding colonies. In some animal populations, younger group members step in to take over some of the duties of their elders without completely displacing them from their positions of power. Old female baboons sit out foraging trips, keeping watch against danger to their families. Old lionesses can survive, sometimes for many years, under the care and feeding provided by their younger pride mates.

When death comes in the animal world, for some it brings bereavement in its wake. Canada geese mate for life, and if one of a pair dies, its mate will mourn dramatically, lowering its head and refusing to defend itself against attack. Lions have been known to remain with the dead body of another lion, licking its fur. Elephants will gather around an ill or fallen herd member and try to raise it to its feet or place food in its mouth. And after it dies, they remain standing by, stroking the dead body with their tusks. Scientists have speculated that elephants have some conception of death based on how keenly they are drawn to elephant bones, although not to bones of other animals. They will sniff and roll bones of their own kind, stroke and examine them, even pick them up and carry them for a time. When a female elephant

Green sea turtle, Sea of Cortez, Mexico

Left by their mother two months earlier to incubate and hatch, baby green sea turtles emerge from their nest buried deep in the sand. In darkness, they make their perilous journey to the sea. Of the 75 to 200 eggs in this clutch, few turtles will survive to maturity. Many will fall victim to predation, and some will drown after becoming trapped in fishing and shrimping trawls. Those that do survive to maturity will mate between the ages of 20 and 50 years. Females will return to nest on the same beaches where they were born years before, beaches that have been used by the turtles for thousands of years.

jaw was brought into camp for study by scientists, her family, passing through the camp, made

a detour to examine the bone. Long after the other elephants moved on, her seven-year-old calf

remained behind, touching it and turning it over and over. Primates have been known to carry

their dead young around with them, unwilling to let them go, loudly decrying the loss with

shrieks and moans. Primatologist Jane Goodall discovered that some primates even seem

to die of grief.

All of life is renewed through the birth of offspring and continues through

procreation, aging, and death. Many animals live only to create new life, and they die at the

completion of mating. The female black widow spider kills and eats her mate, unless he

escapes. By providing a good meal for the female, the male contributes to the welfare of his

offspring. Others, like the mayfly, hatch, mate, lay their eggs, and die, all in a single day.

Under fresh mounds of gravel, below the waterline, new life is forming—the

sockeye salmon's eggs are maturing. Nearby, the riverbank is littered with carcasses of dead

adult salmon. After the scavengers have had their fill, the decomposing bacteria go to work

on the remains of the fish, turning them into a rich food source that will feed another generation

of animals. In death, the salmon contribute to their own and other species' survival, a renewal

of the circle of life.

African lion, Kenya
Lions may live 10 to 15 years in the wild. Weak and toothless, old lions no longer join in the hunt, but they are often allowed to feed on kills made by younger pride members.

Coyote, Wyoming

Death to one animal can mean life to a host of others. A coyote feeds his litter of pups as a raven satisfies the demands of its nest full of fledglings. Even ants, beetles, and flies are nourished by the remains of this bison.

Following spread:

African elephant, Tanzania

The world's largest land mammal may also be the longest lived. Generally, though, the older a bull, the more detached it becomes from the herd. Wrinkled skin, slow locomotion, and sometimes extreme irritability are signs of old age. An aging elephant's heavy, long tusks, once a common sign of longevity, remain a target of ivory poachers, despite international bans.

Factboxes

Page 1 **Mandrill**

Mandrillus sphinx

Size: Up to 30 in. length; 60 lb.

Breeding: Single young born after 220- to 270-day gestation.

Traits: Very colorful face. Scent glands in chest. Short stubby tail. Doglike head. Diurnal. Lives in multimale troops of up to 50 individuals. Facial expressions are important communication tools.

Related Species: Drill.

Endangered: Yes.

Distribution: West Africa.

Conservation Efforts: CITES listing,* habitat preservation, regulated hunting.

Kevin Schafer & Martha Hill

Pages 2–3 **Gray wolf**

Canis lupus

Size: Up to 32 in. height; 175 lb.

Breeding: Thought to mate for life. Single pair in a pack will breed each year. Four to seven pups born and cared for by parents and other pack members.

Traits: Also called timber wolf. As pup grows it either leaves the pack or remains as helper. Omnivorous.

Related Species: Coyote and jackal.

Endangered: Some local distinct subspecies are considered endangered, and others threatened.

Distribution: Europe, Asia, and North America.

Conservation Efforts: Habitat preservation, regulated hunting.

Lynn M. Stone

Pages 4–5 **Northern carmine bee eater**

Merops nubicus

Size: 13.75 in.

Breeding: Nesting hole is dug in the ground and two to six white eggs are laid on a hard surface of regurgitated, undigestible insect material. Young are tended and fed by parents as well as the nonbreeding adults.

Traits: Brightly colored. Eats flying insects (80 percent bees) caught in flight. Pointed, curved beaks, pointed wings, and short legs.

Related Species: 23 species of bee eaters.

Endangered: No.

Distribution: Grasslands of Africa.

Conservation Efforts: Wildlife protection and conservation acts, habitat preservation.

Kevin Schafer

Pages 6–7 **Topi**

Damaliscus lunatus

Size: 3.5-4 ft.;190–300 lb.

Breeding: Breed annually in traditional breeding areas with an eight-month gestation.

Traits: Medium-sized antelope that eats almost exclusively grass. High vantage points are used to display territory and to alert others to danger.

Related Species: 23 species of grazing antelope.

Endangered: Vulnerable.

Distribution: Grasslands of eastern and southern Africa.

Conservation Efforts: Habitat preservation, regulated hunting.

Alan & Sandy Carey

Pages10–11 **African cheetah**

Acinonyx jubatus

Size: About 55 in. length excluding tail; 86–140 lb.

Breeding: Two to four kittens born after 95-day gestation. Kittens often fall prey to lions or hyenas.

Traits: The fastest land animal in the world, adult is able to reach 60 mph. Female hunts alone by day, and male hunts in family groups.

Related Species: Northern Iran cheetah

Endangered: Yes. Asiatic cheetah extinct in India.

Distribution: Northern Iran and sub-Saharan Africa.

Conservation Efforts: CITES listing, wildlife protection and conservation acts, wildlife reserves in native habitat.

Tim Davis and Renee Lynn

Art Wolfe

Pages 12–13 **Gray wolf**

Canis lupus

Size: Up to 32 in. height; 175 lb.

Breeding: Thought to mate for life. Single pair in a pack will breed each year. Four to seven pups born and cared for by parents and other pack members.

Traits: Also called timber wolf. Travels in pack and establishes territories of 40–400 square miles. As pup grows it to leaves the pack or remains as helper. Omnivorous.

Related Species: Coyote and jackal.

Endangered: Some local distinct subspecies are considered endangered, and others threatened.

Distribution: Europe, Asia, and North America.

Conservation Efforts: Habitat preservation, regulated hunting.

Doug Perrine/Innerspace Visions

Pages 14–15 **Atlantic spotted dolphin**

Stenella plagiodon

Size: 7–8.5 ft.

Breeding: Gestation at least 10 months. Single calf born tail first. Calf suckled 8–16 months.

Traits: Feeds on fish and squid. Sleeps resting on the water's surface with one eye open, alternating eyes.

Related Species: 32 dolphin species.

Endangered: No.

Distribution: Tropical Atlantic only.

Conservation Efforts: Marine wildlife conservation acts, fishing net legislation.

Thomas Kitchin/Tom Stack & Assoc.

Pages 16–17 **Bobcat**

Lynx rufus

Size: 25–42 in. length; 20–24 in. height; 13–30 lb.

Breeding: Late-winter breeding. Litters of one to six kittens born after two-month gestation.

Traits: Excellent hearing and vision. Feeds mostly on rabbits, but also rats, squirrels, birds, and even small deer. Primarily nocturnal. Can run up to 30 mph.

Related Species: 36 species of wild cats.

Endangered: No.

Distribution: United States, southern Canada, and central Mexico.

Conservation Efforts: Habitat preservation, regulated hunting, wildlife import and export controls.

Gerry Ellis/ENP Images

Pages 18–19 **Ring-tailed lemur**

Lemur catta

Size: 15–18 in. with 22–24 in. tail; 4–7 lb.

Breeding: Mates in autumn, the single breeding season of the year, with one to four young born in late winter.

Traits: Only lemur with a striped tail. Tail used as a balancing tool. Baby carried in mother's mouth until it is able to cling to her back or stomach fur.

Related Species: 10 species of Lemuridae family.

Endangered: Yes.

Distribution: Madagascar.

Conservation Efforts: CITES listing, habitat preservation.

Tim Davis and Renee Lynn

Pages 20–21 **Japanese macaque**

Macaca fuscata

Size: 2–4 ft. length; up to 33 lb.

Breeding: Single young born after five- to six-month gestation. Long infant dependency period.

Traits: Hairless red face. Large troops led by dominant male. Males ranked by strength. Seldom aggressive. Highly social and territorial.

Related Species: 19 species of macaques.

Endangered: Yes.

Distribution: Japan.

Conservation Efforts: CITES listing, wildlife reserves in native habitat, reforestation efforts.

* Convention on International Trade in Endangered Species of Wild Flora and Fauna.

Pages 22–23 **African lion**

Panthera leo

Size: 6–8 ft. plus 23–35 in. tail; 3 ft. height; 270–500 lb.

Breeding: One to three cubs born after gestation of 100–120 days.

Traits: Carnivorous. Lion family group called a pride. Strongly territorial.

Related Species: Asiatic lion.

Endangered: Vulnerable.

Distribution: Sub-Saharan Africa and India.

Conservation Efforts: Wildlife reserves in native habitat, captive breeding programs.

Rich Kirchner

Kennan Ward

Pages 32–33 **Polar bear**

Ursus maritimus

Size: 5 ft. height; 8–11 ft. length; 660–1,200 lb.

Breeding: Mating from March–June. Two cubs born after gestation of seven to eight months.

Traits: Carnivorous. Solitary but sometimes feed together. Cubs stay with mothers for three years.

Related Species: Brown bear.

Endangered: Vulnerable.

Distribution: Southern Arctic ice cap.

Conservation Efforts: Habitat preservation, regulated hunting.

Page 25 **Greater flamingo**

Phoenicopterus ruber

Size: 4–5 ft.; 55–65 in. wingspan; 6–7 lb.

Breeding: Single offspring hatched after month-long incubation. Incubation duties shared by parents.

Traits: Pairs build mud nests together. Nesting colonies of thousands of birds. Most widespread of the flamingos.

Related Species: The lesser flamingo, Caribbean flamingo, and Andean flamingo.

Endangered: No.

Distribution: Southern Europe, Asia, Africa, West Indies, and Galápagos Islands.

Conservation Efforts: Habitat preservation, restrictions against low-flying aircraft.

Gerry Ellis/ENP Images

Art Wolfe

Pages 34–35 **American bison**

Bison bison

Size: 6 ft. height; up to 2,000 lb.

Breeding: Breeding season is July and August. Single calf is produced after gestation of nine months.

Traits: Bulls travel in bachelor groups except during breeding season. Cows and calves travel in herds.

Related Species: Wisent.

Endangered: No.

Distribution: North America.

Conservation Efforts: Wildlife reserves in native habitat, have increased in numbers this century—from about 500 to perhaps 50,000—on refuges and ranches.

Pages 26–27 **Nile crocodile**

Crocodylus niloticus

Size: 16–18 ft. length; up to 1,500 lb.

Breeding: Mating occurs late in the year. Eggs, 50–80 at a time, are buried near but not in water. Incubation is 2.5–3 months.

Traits: Large communities ranging from a few dozen to a few hundred individuals. Rarely venture far from the water.

Related Species: 12 species of *Crocodylus*.

Endangered: Vulnerable.

Distribution: Sub-Saharan Africa, Nile, Madagascar.

Conservation Efforts: Habitat preservation, regulated hunting, wildlife import and export controls.

Roger de la Harpe

Mark Wallner

Pages 36–37 **White-tailed deer**

Odocoileus virginianus

Size: 1.8–3.6 ft. height; 300–450 lb.

Breeding: Breed November–January. Often have twins.

Traits: Most abundant large game species in North America. Can run up to 40 mph and live up to 16 years. Raises tail when running.

Related Species: Deer, moose, elk, and caribou.

Endangered: No.

Distribution: Southern Canada, throughout the United States, and south to Bolivia.

Conservation Efforts: Cutting of climax forests, regulated hunting.

Page 29 **Brown bear**

Ursus arctos

Size: 5–7 ft.; 600–800 lb. average.

Breeding: Birth of twin cubs in January–March after a gestation of 180–266 days while the female is hibernating.

Traits: The largest living carnivore, acute smell and hearing. Poor eyesight. Generally solitary. Only social bonds seem to be between mother and cubs.

Related Species: Black bear and polar bear.

Endangered: Threatened.

Distribution: Europe, Palestine to eastern Siberia, the Himalaya, Africa, Japan, Alaska, western Canada, and possibly northern Mexico.

Conservation Efforts: Habitat preservation, regulated hunting.

Art Wolfe

Kim Taylor/Bruce Coleman Ltd.

Page 38 **Scaffold web spider**

Enoplognatha ovata

Size: 0.5 in.

Breeding: Female guards grayish-blue egg sac, which is enclosed in a curled leaf. Female does not live long enough to see eggs hatch.

Traits: Seemingly fearless. Will attack any insect regardless of size. Flings sticky threads over prey from a distance then bites, injecting venom.

Related Species: House spider family.

Endangered: No.

Distribution: Europe and North America.

Conservation Efforts: Habitat preservation.

Page 30 **Japanese macaque**

Macaca fuscata

Size: 2–4 ft. length; up to 33 lb.

Breeding: Single young born after five- to six-month gestation. Long infant dependency period.

Traits: Hairless red face. Large troops led by dominant male. Males ranked by strength. Seldom aggressive. Highly social and territorial.

Related Species: 19 species of macaques.

Endangered: Yes.

Distribution: Japan.

Conservation Efforts: CITES listing, wildlife reserves in native habitat, habitat preservation.

Art Wolfe

Kevin Schafer

Page 39 **Three-toed sloth**

Bradypus variegatus

Size: 20–27 in.; 9–20 lb.

Breeding: Mates in treetops. Single young born after five to six months and cared for by mother alone.

Traits: Leaf-eating and arboreal. Nocturnal and solitary.

Related Species: Anteater and armadillo.

Endangered: Yes, some subspecies.

Distribution: Central and South American rainforests.

Conservation Efforts: CITES listing, habitat preservation.

Pages 40–41 **Arctic fox**

Alopex lagopus

Size: 25.5–33.5 in.; 5.5–11 lb.

Breeding: Five to eight or more kits in litter. Gestation of six to eight weeks.

Traits: Burrows into side of hill or cliff. Feeds on ground-dwelling birds or rodents or the leftovers of larger predators. Does not hibernate.

Related Species: Other vulpine foxes.

Endangered: No.

Distribution: Arctic regions of Europe, Asia, and North America.

Conservation Efforts: Regulated hunting.

Tom and Pat Leeson

Pages 42–43 **Killer whale**

Orcinus orca

Size: Up to 25–30 ft.; 6–10 tons.

Breeding: Female gives birth once every five years to single offspring weighing about 400 pounds after a gestation of 17 months. Calf nurses for a year.

Traits: Swims in pods of 5–30 members. Fastest swimming marine mammal. Consumes more than 100 pounds a day of fish, squid, and marine mammals.

Related Species: Toothed whales, bottlenose dolphin, and pilot whale.

Endangered: No.

Distribution: Worldwide, usually within 500 miles of shore.

Conservation Efforts: Protected by International Whaling Commission.

Jeff Foott

Page 44 **Giraffe**

Giraffa camelopardalis

Size: 12–17 ft.; up to 2,750 lb.

Breeding: Single calf born after 14-month gestation.

Traits: Loosely bound herds with female spending just over half its time browsing for food, male slightly less. Communal child care. May live over 30 years.

Related Species: Nine subspecies and the rare okapi.

Endangered: No.

Distribution: Sub-Saharan Africa.

Conservation Efforts: Wildlife reserves in native habitat, protected herds in Serengeti National Park increasing at 5 percent a year.

Tim Davis and Renee Lynn

Page 45 **African cheetah**

Acinonyx jubatus

Size: About 55 in. length excluding tail; 110–130 lb.

Breeding: Two to four kittens born after 95-day gestation. Poor survival rate among kittens, who often fall prey to lions or hyenas.

Traits: The fastest land animal in the world, adult is able to reach 60 mph. Female hunts by day alone and male hunts in family group.

Related Species: Northern Iran cheetah.

Endangered: Yes. Asiatic cheetah exterminated in India.

Distribution: East and central Africa and northern Iran.

Conservation Efforts: CITES listing, habitat preservation.

Gerry Ellis/ENP Images

Pages 46–47 **Red-fronted lemur**

Eulemur fulvus rufus

Size: 16 in.; 22 in. tail; 6 lb.

Breeding: One young born per year in the fall after 120-day gestation.

Traits: Permanent groups of seven to eight animals on average. Social bonds established and reinforced through grooming. Feeds on branches, sap, leaves, pods, and stems of kily tree.

Related Species: 6 other subspecies of brown lemurs.

Endangered: Threatened.

Distribution: Madagascar.

Conservation Efforts: Habitat preservation.

Tom and Pat Leeson

Art Wolfe

Pages 48–49 **African elephant**

Loxodonta africana

Size: 10 ft. shoulder height; 3–6 tons.

Breeding: No particular breeding time. Single calf born after 22-month gestation.

Traits: Herbivorous. Female lives in matriarchal herd. Young male lives in bachelor herd. Adult male is solitary. Highly social with strong family ties.

Related Species: Asian elephant.

Endangered: Yes.

Distribution: Sub-Saharan Africa.

Conservation Efforts: CITES listing, wildlife reserves in native habitat, hunting bans on ivory.

Tom and Pat Leeson

Page 50 **Hippopotamus**

Hippopotamus amphibius

Size: 11 ft. length; 2.5–3.5 tons.

Breeding: Single young born after 200-day gestation. Young sometimes born underwater.

Traits: Live in groups of 15–20 near small bodies of water. Territory patrolled by dominant male. Forages for food at night. Herbivorous. Spends most of day in water. Exceeded in size only by elephant.

Related Species: Pygmy hippo.

Endangered: No.

Distribution: Eastern and central Africa.

Conservation Efforts: Habitat preservation and hunting bans.

C. Gable Ray

Page 51 **Pileated woodpecker**

Dryocopus pileatus

Size: 16–17 in. length.

Breeding: Four eggs on average incubated 12–14 days. Parents take turns incubating.

Traits: Largest woodpecker in North America. Feeds on insects, fruit, and nuts. Hollows out nest 2 feet deep and 8 inches wide.

Related Species: Black woodpecker.

Endangered: No.

Distribution: North America.

Conservation Efforts: Wildlife protection and conservation acts.

Jeff Foott

Pages 52–53 **Trumpeter swan**

Cygnus buccinator

Size: 5.5 ft. length; 10 ft. wingspan.

Breeding: An average of six pale eggs are laid on ground nests. Male guards the eggs. Cygnet can run and swim within hours of hatching.

Traits: Named for its low-pitched call. Sociable except during breeding season. Mates for life. Fastest waterfowl on water or in the air. Feeds on aquatic plants in shallow waters.

Related Species: 7 species of swans.

Endangered: Vulnerable.

Distribution: North America.

Conservation Efforts: Wildlife reserves in native habitat.

Gerry Ellis/ENP Images

Pages 54–55 **Orangutan**

Pongo pygmaeus

Size: 3–4 ft.; 90–200 lb.

Breeding: Single young born after gestation of 260–270 days. Twins occur but are rare.

Traits: Most solitary of the apes. Lives in rainforest treetops, with female and young rarely descending to the ground. Active during daylight seeking nuts, leaves, insects, and eggs to eat.

Related Species: Sumatran and Bornean orangutans.

Endangered: Yes.

Distribution: Borneo and Sumatra.

Conservation Efforts: CITES listing, wildlife import and export controls.

Page 56 **Wolf spider**

Aracneae lycosidae

Size: 0.75–1.15 in.

Breeding: Female carries large egg sac. After hatching, spiderlings climb on mother's back.

Traits: Vagabond lifestyle. Hunts its prey not with webs but with a sit-and-wait strategy. Feeds on insects smaller than itself.

Related Species: 2,500 species of wolf spiders.

Endangered: No.

Distribution: North America.

Conservation Efforts: Habitat preservation.

Robert and Linda Mitchell

Daniel J. Cox

Pages 62–63 **Humpback whale**

Megaptera novaeangliae

Size: 39–49 ft.; up to 10 tons.

Breeding: Breeding takes place every two to three years. Gestation of 12–13 months. Young nurse for 11 months.

Traits: Elaborate feeding and courtship behaviors. Lives in groups and migrates seasonally between polar and tropical waters.

Related Species: Minke, Bryde's, sei, fin, and blue whales.

Endangered: Vulnerable.

Distribution: Atlantic, Arctic, and Pacific Oceans, the waters of the Bering Sea and the waters surrounding Antarctica.

Conservation Efforts: Protected by International Whaling Commission.

Page 57 **Giant water bug**

Abedus sp.

Size: 1–2 in.

Breeding: Mates in spring and early summer. Female lays eggs and cements them to dorsal surface of the male. Eggs grow quickly during the summer.

Traits: Inhabits ponds and streams. Legs are adapted for swimming and prey capture. Mouthparts used for piercing and sucking.

Related Species: 3,200 species of aquatic or semiaquatic water bugs.

Endangered: No.

Distribution: North and Central America.

Conservation Efforts: Habitat preservation.

Robert and Linda Mitchell

Walt Enders/ENP Images

Page 65 **King penguin**

Aptenodytes patagonicus

Size: 37 in.; 20–33 lb.

Breeding: Nests in huge colonies on beaches or valleys free of snow and ice. Male incubates eggs (62–66 days) while female leaves to feed. Male fasts throughout courtship, mating period, and incubation.

Traits: The most social of all birds. Usually forages in water over shelf and slope areas.

Related Species: 17 species of penguins.

Endangered: No.

Distribution: Sub-Antarctic islands and peninsulas.

Conservation Efforts: Marine wildlife conservation acts.

Page 58 **Pygmy marsupial frog**

Flectonotus pygmaeus

Size: Up to 0.87 in.

Breeding: Breeds in rainy season. Female lays 10 eggs, which are fertilized by male and then reinserted into the female's pouch to be carried by her until tadpoles are released.

Traits: Nocturnal. Belongs to the largest family of frogs, the tree frogs. Frogs utilize shorter hind legs and a lever system for jumping. The tadpole phase distinguishes frogs among amphibians.

Related Species: *Gastrotheca marsupiata.*

Endangered: No.

Distribution: Venezuela and Colombia.

Conservation Efforts: Habitat preservation, wildlife import and export controls.

M. & P. Fogden/Bruce Coleman Ltd.

Richard Herrmann/Innerspace Visions

Page 67 **Blue shark**

Prionace glauca

Size: Up to 13 ft. length; 100 lb. average.

Breeding: Pups born (25–50 at a time) after gestation of 9–12 months.

Traits: Feeds primarily on schooling fish. One of the most common and wide-ranging sharks with complex migratory habits. Solitary. Has been called the "perfect predator."

Related Species: 350 other sharks.

Endangered: No.

Distribution: Oceanic Islands, Atlantic Ocean, Pacific Ocean, Indian Ocean.

Conservation Efforts: Marine wildlife conservation acts, fishing restrictions.

Page 59 **Capybara**

Hydrochaeris hydrochaeris

Size: 24 in. height; up to 50 in. length; 80–140 lb. Head may be as large as a bull's.

Breeding: Three to eight young produced each year after 150-day gestation.

Traits: Semiaquatic, herbivorous. Largest rodent in world. Shy, associates in groups on riverbanks. Feeds in morning and evening.

Related Species: One other semiaquatic water hog of South and Central America.

Endangered: No.

Distribution: South America.

Conservation Efforts: Annual hunt in Venezuela is regulated by government.

Art Wolfe

Tim Davis and Renee Lynn

Page 68 **Gerenuk**

Litocranius walleri

Size: 56–64 in. length; 64–114 lb.

Breeding: Breeds year-round. Single young born after gestation of seven months.

Traits: Diurnal. Habitat is dry scrub areas. Travels in small groups or alone. Feeds on leaves and bushes. Drinks rarely, if at all, as it does not require water.

Related Species: Suni, oribi, and duiker antelope.

Endangered: No.

Distribution: Africa.

Conservation Efforts: Wildlife protection and conservation acts, wildlife reserves in native habitat.

Pages 60–61 **Mountain goat**

Oreamnos americanus

Size: 4–6 ft. length; 100–300 lb.

Breeding: Single young is born (twins or triplets rarely) in May or June after 150- to 180-day gestation. Young often snatched by eagles.

Traits: Loosely associated small bands. Female shows strong loyalty to home range, while male wanders widely. Herbivorous. Surefooted, makes its way to highest spot in area.

Related Species: Desert bighorn sheep.

Endangered: No.

Distribution: Western North America.

Conservation Efforts: Regulated hunting, logging limits.

Art Wolfe

Doug Perrine/Innerspace Visions

Page 70 **Lionfish**

Pterois volitans

Size: 15 in.

Breeding: Not observed in the wild.

Traits: Spines have venom glands for defense only. The effects on humans from fish's sting can last for months. Inhabits coral reefs, shallow water areas. Coloring serves as camouflage among coral.

Related Species: Stonefish and scorpionfish proper.

Endangered: No.

Distribution: Red Sea, Indian Ocean, waters off China, Japan, Australia, Melanesia, Micronesia, and Polynesia.

Conservation Efforts: Marine wildlife conservation acts, wildlife import and export controls.

Page 71 Prairie falcon

Falco mexicanus

Size: 19.5 in.; 36–44 in. wingspan.

Breeding: Clutch size four to five eggs. Nests often on ledges.

Traits: Forages for birds and small mammals. Short-distance migrations.

Related Species: Sharp-shinned hawk, American kestrel, and merlin.

Endangered: No.

Distribution: Parts of Canada, United States, and northern Mexico.

Conservation Efforts: Migratory bird protection acts.

Art Wolfe

Tom and Pat Leeson

Pages 78–79 Eurasian lynx

Lynx lynx

Size: 2.5–4 ft. length; 40–44 lb.

Breeding: Mates in early spring. One to five young born after gestation of 70 days.

Traits: Shy, secretive. Young remain in trees. Does not hibernate. Acute hearing used to hunt. Large feet serve as snowshoes.

Related Species: Canada lynx.

Endangered: Vulnerable.

Distribution: Europe and Siberia.

Conservation Efforts: Habitat preservation, regulated hunting.

Pages 72–73 **Atlantic puffin**

Fratercula arctica

Size: 12 in.

Breeding: Single egg incubated for six to seven weeks.

Traits: Also called a sea parrot. Nests on coastal islands. Feeds on small pelagic fish. Winters at sea. Tricolored beak brightens in mating season.

Related Species: Horned puffin, tufted puffin.

Endangered: Threatened.

Distribution: Northern Atlantic, from southern Greenland and Iceland to New England and the British Isles.

Conservation Efforts: Migratory bird protection acts, wildlife reserves in native habitat.

Pete Oxford/ENP Images

Kevin Schafer

Pages 80–81 African lion

Panthera leo

Size: Up to 6–8 ft. length with 23–35 in. tail; 3 ft. height at shoulder; 270–500 lb.

Breeding: One to three cubs born after gestation of 100–120 days.

Traits: Carnivorous. Family group called a pride. Strongly territorial. Hunts at night.

Related Species: Several *Panthera* species.

Endangered: Vulnerable.

Distribution: Sub-Saharan Africa and India.

Conservation Efforts: Wildlife reserves in native habitat, captive breeding programs.

Pages 74–75 **Hog-nosed viper**

Porthidium nasutum

Size: 18–24 in.

Breeding: After mating, fertilized eggs with leathery shells are deposited by female in a shallow hole.

Traits: Extremely venomous member of viper family. Fangs are carried folded and are erected when preparing to bite.

Related Species: 200 species of the viper family.

Endangered: No.

Distribution: Central America, Colombia, and Ecuador.

Conservation Efforts: Wildlife protection and conservation acts, wildlife import and export controls.

Steve Kaufman

Brian Kenney

Page 82 Chinese mantid

Tenodera aridifolia

Size: 3–4 in. length

Breeding: The female lays 100–300 eggs in an egg case and then attaches the case to twigs or branches. Male is decapitated by female during or after mating.

Traits: Eye color changes at night to facilitate night hunting. Prefers flowering plants as camouflage. Cleans front legs (which capture and hold prey) and antennae after eating.

Related Species: 1,800 mantid species.

Endangered: No.

Distribution: East Asia and North America.

Conservation Efforts: Habitat preservation, wildlife import and export controls.

Page 76 Common octopus

Octopus vulgaris

Size: Up to 10 ft.; up to 55 lb.

Breeding: One week after mating 150,000 eggs laid of which just over one percent will hatch in four to six weeks. Female usually dies after breeding.

Traits: Solitary, bottom-dwelling. Feeds on crabs, crayfish, bivalves. Eight legs used for swimming, holding prey, fighting, housebuilding, and breeding.

Related Species: Squid, cuttlefish, and nautilus.

Endangered: No.

Distribution: Warm waters worldwide.

Conservation Efforts: Marine wildlife conservation acts, fishing restrictions.

Doug Perrine/Innerspace Visions

Erwin and Peggy Bauer

Page 83 Shoebill stork

Balaeniceps rex

Size: 3.5 ft. length

Breeding: One to two eggs laid in ground nest of grasses and reeds. Parents share incubation duties.

Traits: Large shovel-like bill used for foraging in the mud. Feeds on frogs, snakes, mollusks, carrion. Solitary.

Related Species: Stork family (disputed).

Endangered: No.

Distribution: East central Africa

Conservation Efforts: Habitat preservation.

Page 77 **Henkel's leaf-tailed gecko**

Uroplatus henkeli

Size: 3–12 in.

Breeding: Two eggs laid, only one of which will hatch 70–130 days later.

Traits: Patterning on body takes after plants in the area. Highly sociable, nocturnal.

Related Species: 10 species of Uroplatidae.

Endangered: No.

Distribution: Madagascar.

Conservation Efforts: Habitat preservation.

Brian Kenney

Brandon D. Cole/ENP Images

Pages 84–85 Sunflower sea star

Pycnopodia helianthoides

Size: 19–31 in. diameter.

Breeding: March–July breeding. Sperm and eggs released into the water where they join by chance. Larval period is 2–10 weeks.

Traits: The largest of the Pacific Coast sea stars with 15–24 arms. Feeds on a wide range of crustaceans or dying fish. Color changes to hide from predators. Usually antagonistic with other stars.

Related Species: Mud star, brittle star.

Endangered: No.

Distribution: Alaska to Baja California, Mexico.

Conservation Efforts: Marine wildlife conservation acts.

Pages 86–87 **Nile crocodile**

Crocodylus niloticus

Size: 16–18 ft. length; up to 1,500 lb.

Breeding: Mates late in the year. Eggs, 50–80 at a time, are buried near but not in water. Incubation is 2.5–3 months.

Traits: Large communities ranging from a few dozen to a few hundred individuals. Rarely ventures far from the water.

Related Species: 12 species of *Crocodylus*.

Endangered: Vulnerable.

Distribution: Sub-Saharan Africa, the Nile, and Madagascar.

Conservation Efforts: Habitat preservation, regulated hunting, and wildlife import and export controls.

Thomas De Soto

Orion Service and Trading Co. Inc./
Bruce Coleman Ltd.

Pages 94–95 **Japanese crane**

Grus japonensis

Size: 4–5 ft.; 7–8 ft. wingspan.

Breeding: Nest made of reeds and grasses. Two eggs (rarely one or three) are incubated over a month by both parents, who switch places 2–10 times a day.

Traits: Families remain together nine months. Grown young are chased away just before breeding season. Migratory. Feeds on mud fishes and vegetable matter.

Related Species: European, black-necked, hooded, sandhill, whooping, white-naped, sarus, Australian, and Siberian white cranes.

Endangered: Vulnerable.

Distribution: Siberia to Japan, winters in Hokkaido, Japan.

Conservation Efforts: Migratory bird protection acts, habitat preservation, captive release programs.

Page 88 **Six-spotted fishing spider**

Dolomedes triton

Size: 0.4–0.5 in.

Breeding: Egg sac produced June to September. Female carries it across open water and remains close until spiderlings hatch and disperse.

Traits: Does not make webs. Feeds on insects, salamanders, and small fish. Propels itself across water surface using its legs. One of few spiders to adapt to aquatic habitat.

Related Species: Nursery web spider.

Endangered: No.

Distribution: Canada and United States.

Conservation Efforts: Habitat preservation.

Brian Kenney

Steve Drogin/Innerspace Visions

Page 97 **Atlantic spotted dolphin**

Stenella plagiodon

Size: 7–8.5 ft.

Breeding: Gestation at least 10 months. Single calf born tail first. Calf suckled 8–16 months.

Traits: Feeds on fish and squid. Sleeps resting on the water's surface with one eye open, alternating eyes. High mortality rate in first two years of life.

Related Species: 32 dolphin species.

Endangered: No.

Distribution: Tropical Atlantic only.

Conservation Efforts: Marine wildlife conservation acts, fishing net legislation.

Page 89 **Wandering spider**

Cupiennius sp.

Size: Up to 1.5 in.

Breeding: Female carries egg sac on abdomen until eggs hatch and spiderlings disperse.

Traits: Actively searches for prey.

Related Species: Swamp and wolf spiders.

Endangered: No.

Distribution: Worldwide.

Conservation Efforts: Habitat preservation.

Michael Fogden

Erwin and Peggy Bauer

Pages 98–99 **Coyote**

Canis latrans

Size: 40–46 in. length; 19–30 lb. average.

Breeding: One to six young born early spring after gestation of 60–63 days. Male brings food to mate while awaiting the pups' birth. Pairs mate for life.

Traits: Hunts individually or in pairs. Nocturnal. Uses same den year after year. Most vocal of all North American wild carnivores. Acute hearing and sense of smell. Good swimmer.

Related Species: Domestic dog, wolf.

Endangered: No.

Distribution: North and Central America.

Conservation Efforts: Habitat preservation, regulated hunting.

Pages 90–91 **Giant panda**

Ailuropoda melanoleuca

Size: 5–6 ft.; 200–300 lb.

Breeding: One or two young born at a time. Tiny cubs are only 5 ounces at birth.

Traits: Feeds on bamboo shoots, leaves, and stems.

Related Species: None known.

Endangered: Yes.

Distribution: Western and southwestern China.

Conservation Efforts: CITES listing, captive breeding programs, wildlife reserves in native habitat.

Tom and Pat Leeson

David M. Dennis/Tom Stack
& Assoc.

Page 101 **Red-spotted newt**

Notophthalmus viridescens

Size: 1–4 in.

Breeding: Breeds late winter to early spring. Eggs attached to underwater vegetation. Brown larvae emerge from eggs several days later.

Traits: Found in shallow ponds, slow-moving rivers and streams. Mating behavior of adult salamander includes "dancing" by male throughout the night. Prefers water not deep enough to contain fish. Carnivorous.

Related Species: 53 newt species.

Endangered: No.

Distribution: Eastern United States.

Conservation Efforts: Habitat preservation.

Pages 92–93 **Bald eagle**

Haliaeetus leucocephalus

Size: 3 ft.; 6 ft. wingspan; 7–10 lb.

Breeding: One or two eggs hatch in five to six weeks.

Traits: Nests in top of tall trees near water. Returns to same aerie (nest) every year. Hunts during day. Feeds mainly on fish; snatching them while flying. May eat other birds, mammals, and carrion. United States' national bird since 1782.

Related Species: Golden eagle.

Endangered: Threatened.

Distribution: North America.

Conservation Efforts: Wildlife protection and conservation acts, pesticide bans.

Tom and Pat Leeson

Kevin Schafer

Page 102 **Guanaco**

Lama guanicoe

Size: 42 in. shoulder height; 250–300 lb.

Breeding: Gestation of 11 months. Young born December–February. Nurse 11–15 months. Male mates with several females.

Traits: Herbivorous. Social groups are family groups, male troops, and solitary males. Male defends territory. Adult can run up to 35 mph.

Related Species: Alpaca llama.

Endangered: Vulnerable.

Distribution: South America from southern Peru southward, and far western Paraguay.

Conservation Efforts: Habitat preservation, regulated hunting.

Pages 104–105 **Market squid**

Loligo opalescene

Size: 7.5–19.5 in.

Breeding: Male fertilizes female, which lays hundreds of eggs at night in capsules that are attached to something solid on the ocean floor. Eggs hatch in 30 days. Parents do not guard or care for eggs.

Traits: Feeds on small fish. Fast, long-distance swimmer. Congregates in schools. Occupies shallow coastal waters.

Related Species: Other species of the genus *Loligo* in North America and Europe.

Endangered: No.

Distribution: Eastern Pacific Ocean.

Conservation Efforts: Marine wildlife conservation acts.

Jeff Foott

Page 106 **Siberian tiger**

Panthera tigris altaica

Size: 9–12 ft. length; 400–800 lb.

Breeding: No particular mating season. Up to six cubs born after gestation of 3–3.5 months.

Traits: Carnivorous. Female lives in a family, male is solitary. Mostly nocturnal. Occupies large territories.

Related Species: Bengal and Sumatran tigers.

Endangered: Yes.

Distribution: Amur-Ussuri region of Siberia, northern China, and Korea.

Conservation Efforts: CITES listing, wildlife reserves in native habitat.

Konrad Wothe/ENP Images

Page 107 **Red-eyed tree frog**

Agalychnis callidryas

Size: 2–3 in.

Breeding: From 30 to 50 eggs deposited on underside of leaf overhanging water. After hatching five days later, tadpoles fall into water.

Traits: Carnivorous. Catch prey with sticky tongue and swallow prey whole. Adhesive toe pads stick to leaves or vertical surfaces.

Related Species: Pacific tree frog, gray tree frog, giant tree frog.

Endangered: No.

Distribution: Mexico through Central America.

Conservation Efforts: Habitat preservation.

Kevin Schafer

Page 108 **Black-browed albatross**

Diomedea melanophris

Size: 20–50 in.; 12 ft. wingspan.

Breeding: Single egg is incubated 10–11 weeks in nesting colony near water.

Traits: Most marine of birds. Travels great distances, sleeps on the ocean's surface, and feeds on marine life.

Related Species: 13–14 species of albatross.

Endangered: No.

Distribution: Southern oceans.

Conservation Efforts: Marine wildlife conservation acts.

Kevin Schafer

Page 109 **Grunion**

Leuresthes tenuis

Size: 5–6 in.

Breeding: Eggs burrowed 2–3 inches into the sand by female and fertilized by male. Eggs hatch two weeks later and babies are swept out to sea.

Traits: Small silvery fish that comes out of the water completely to lay its eggs shortly after high tide.

Related Species: Topsmelt, jacksmelt.

Endangered: No.

Distribution: California coast south through Baja California, Mexico.

Conservation Efforts: Fishing restrictions.

Jeff Foott

Gerry Ellis/ENP Images

Pages 110–111 **Great gray bowerbird**

Chlamydera nuchalis

Size: 9–15 in.

Breeding: From one to three eggs laid in deep nest cup. Female works alone to build nest, incubate eggs for 19–24 days, and feed young.

Traits: Male builds elaborate bower up to 9 feet high to be used for courtship displays. The bower's floor and walls are made of small sticks and are decorated with shells and dead insects.

Related Species: 18 species of the family with a possible link to birds of paradise.

Endangered: No.

Distribution: Australia, New Guinea, and nearby islands.

Conservation Efforts: Australia's wildlife protection and conservation acts.

Kevin Schafer

Pages 112–113 **Stick-mimicking grasshopper**

Utropidacris cristata

Size: 1.5–4 in.

Breeding: Lays eggs in an egg pod buried by female. Young hatch as tiny wormlike nymphs, which molt immediately upon hatching.

Traits: Diurnal. Herbivorous. Elongated with conical head.

Related Species: 100 species of Proscopiidae family.

Endangered: No.

Distribution: South America.

Conservation Efforts: Habitat preservation.

Gerry Ellis/ENP Images

Page 114 **Blue peafowl**

Pavo cristatus

Size: Up to 78 in. length.

Breeding: Female incubates four to eight eggs for 27–28 days.

Traits: Member of pheasant family. Nests on the ground or low branches. Feeds mostly on worms, insects, seeds, and small snakes. Tail more than twice the length of body.

Related Species: Green peafowl and Congo peafowl.

Endangered: No.

Distribution: Tropical Asia.

Conservation Efforts: Habitat preservation.

Tim Davis and Renee Lynn

Page 115 **Giraffe**

Giraffa camelopardalis

Size: 12–17 ft.; up to 2,750 lb.

Breeding: Single calf born after 14-month gestation .

Traits: Loosely bound herds with female spending just over half its time browsing for food, male slightly less. Communal child care. May live over 30 years.

Related Species: Nine subspecies and the rare okapi.

Endangered: No.

Distribution: Sub-Saharan Africa.

Conservation Efforts: Wildlife reserves in native habitat, protected herds in Serengeti National Park increasing at 5 percent a year.

Art Wolfe

Page 116 **Black rhinoceros**

Diceros bicornis

Size: 4–5 ft. shoulder height; 1,400–2,800 lb.

Breeding: Single calf born after 15- to 16-month gestation. Breeding and birth peak in rainy months.

Traits: Herbivorous browser. Solitary. Extremely aggressive. Sometimes forms groups. Readily attacks predators. Acute hearing and sense of smell. Bull will mark territory.

Related Species: Southern and northern white rhinoceros.

Endangered: Yes.

Distribution: Zimbabwe and South Africa.

Conservation Efforts: CITES listing, wildlife reserves in native habitat, and captive breeding programs.

Page 117 **Gray angelfish**

Pomacanthus arcuatus

Size: Up to 24 in.

Breeding: Egg scatterer.

Traits: Spectacular coloring. Aggressive toward other angelfish. The young change from black with yellow stripes to primarily gray as adults.

Related Species: Six species of larger angelfish.

Endangered: No.

Distribution: Tropical or reef habitats from New England coast south to Brazil.

Conservation Efforts: Marine wildlife conservation acts, willdlife import and export controls.

Doug Perrine/Innerspace Visions

John Botkin

Pages 126–127 **Bengal tiger**

Panthera tigris tigris

Size: 9–10 ft. length; 36 in. height; 400–575 lb.

Breeding: Breeds in spring with litters of two to four born after 15 weeks.

Traits: Solitary and nocturnal. Carnivorous. Lives up to 15 years. May occupy a home range 20 miles square and eat as much as 65 pounds of meat in a single night.

Related Species: Seven subspecies of *Panthera tigris* (two of which are extinct).

Endangered: Yes.

Distribution: India, Bangladesh, Burma, and Nepal.

Conservation Efforts: CITES listing, habitat preservation, regulated hunting, wildlife reserves in native habitat. Conservation programs have increased numbers to 4,000 from a 1972 low of 1,850.

Pages 118–119 **Plain's zebra**

Equus burchelli

Size: 47–55 in. height; 400–500 lb.

Breeding: Single 70- to 80-pound foal born after gestation of just over one year.

Traits: Small family groups may form mixed, migratory herds with antelopes and wildebeests. Spends 60–80 percent of time eating. Feeds on fruits, grasses, roots, and bark.

Related Species: Grevy's zebra and mountain zebra.

Endangered: No.

Distribution: Eastern and southern Africa.

Conservation Efforts: Captive breeding programs, wildlife reserves in native habitat.

Kevin Schafer

Kevin Schafer

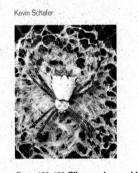

Pages 128–129 **Silver argiope spider**

Argiope argentata

Size: 0.12–0.25 in.

Breeding: Female attaches two to three sacs of several hundred eggs to leaf or branch and then she dies.

Traits: Feeds on insects. The zig-zagging cross strands of the spider's web form an "X" in the web's center.

Related Species: Orb weavers.

Endangered: No.

Distribution: Neotropics and temperate North America.

Conservation Efforts: Habitat preservation.

Pages 120–121 **African elephant**

Loxodonta africana

Size: 10 ft. shoulder height; 3–6 tons.

Breeding: No particular breeding time. Single calf born after gestation of 22 months.

Traits: Herbivorous. Female lives in matriarchal herd. Young male lives in bachelor herd. Adult male is solitary. Highly social with strong family ties.

Related Species: Asian elephant.

Endangered: Yes.

Distribution: Sub-Saharan Africa.

Conservation Efforts: CITES listing, wildlife reserves in native habitat, hunting bans on ivory.

Tom and Pat Leeson

G. C. Kelley/Tom Stack & Assoc.

Page 131 **Elf owl**

Micrathene whitneyi

Size: 5–6 in.; 15 in. wingspan.

Breeding: Mate in May and June. Two to five eggs.

Traits: Smallest owl in North America. Feeds on insects, scorpions, smalls birds, or lizards. Nocturnal. No need for water. Short-distance migrations. Often nests in saguaro cactus.

Related Species: 120 species within the Strigidae family.

Endangered: No.

Distribution: Southwestern United States, northern Mexico, Central America.

Conservation Efforts: Captive breeding programs, habitat preservation.

Pages 122–123 **Parson's chameleon**

Calumma parsonii

Size: 12–14 in.

Breeding: Female deposits clutch of 15–20 eggs underground.

Traits: One of the largest chameleons. Tongue reaches speed of 16.5 feet per second. Eyes rotate independently of each other. Slow-moving. Male has two nose appendages.

Related Species: Panther chameleon.

Endangered: Vulnerable.

Distribution: Madagascar

Conservation Efforts: Wildlife import and export controls.

Erwin and Peggy Bauer

Tom and Pat Leeson

Page 132 **Beaver**

Castor canadensis

Size: 3–4 ft.; 25–55 lb.

Breeding: From two to four young born after gestation of three months. Female has young every two years.

Traits: Largest rodent in world after capybara. Stores food for winter use. Builds elaborate lodges and dams by cutting down trees with teeth that grow throughout its lifetime. Will remain in lodge, adding on and repairing it, as long as there is food in the area.

Related Species: Rodents.

Endangered: Yes, some subspecies.

Distribution: United States, Canada, Europe, and Asia.

Conservation Efforts: CITES listing, habitat preservation.

Pages 124–125 **Red deer**

Cervus elaphus

Size: 4–5 ft. height; 220–260 lb. average.

Breeding: Mates in early fall. Single young born (twins rare) after gestation of 235 days.

Traits: Sociable. Males form separate herds. Herbivorous. May live 20 years. Natural habitat is forest.

Related Species: 23 subspecies of deer.

Endangered: Yes, some subspecies.

Distribution: Scandinavia, Europe, west Africa, Asia Minor, Australia, New Zealand, Argentina, and North America.

Conservation Efforts: CITES listing, habitat preservation.

John Cancalosi/Bruce Coleman Ltd.

Kevin Schafer

Page 135 **White tent bat**

Ectophylla alba

Size: 1–1.5 in.; 0.2 oz.

Breeding: Breeds at other than rainy season. Single young per female.

Traits: Makes tent of plant leaves. Roosts under leaves. Diurnal. Frugivorous. Tent may house up to 12 bats.

Related Species: Other tent-maker bats.

Endangered: No.

Distribution: Central America.

Conservation Efforts: Habitat preservation.

Pages 136–137 **Cleaning shrimp**

Periclemenes sp.

Size: 0.75 in.

Breeding: Thought to be hermaphroditic but cannot fertilize themselves. Sperm packet can be accepted only after molting.

Traits: Transparent body. Lives among tentacles of sea anemone and other sea creatures. Nitrogen released by the shrimp contributes to the photosynthesis of the algae from which anemones derive nutrients.

Related Species: Scarlet cleaning shrimp.

Endangered: No.

Distribution: Indo-Pacific and Red Sea.

Conservation Efforts: Marine wildlife conservation acts.

Doug Perrine/Innerspace Visions

Frank S. Balthis

Pages 144–145 **Antarctic blue-eyed cormorant**

Phalacrocorax atriceps

Size: 27–29 in. length; 43 in. wingspan.

Breeding: Two to four pale blue eggs hatch after three- to five-week incubation.

Traits: Nest is built of seaweed or guano about 50 feet above the high tide line. Underwater swimmer that dives as deep as 300 feet for fish.

Related Species: 32 other species of cormorants.

Endangered: No.

Distribution: Western side of the Antarctic Peninsula, the Scotia Arc, and South Georgia.

Conservation Efforts: Wildlife reserves in native habitat.

Pages 138–139 **Canada goose**

Branta canadensis

Size: 21–43 in.

Breeding: Nests mid-February–late March. Four to seven eggs are laid and incubated for 28 days. Parents share child care.

Traits: Mates for life. Nests near water. Male very territorial and protective of female and goslings. Migrates south flying in V-shape formation. Rich honk.

Related Species: 11 subspecies of Canada Geese

Endangered: No.

Distribution: North America.

Conservation Efforts: Migratory bird protection acts.

Erwin and Peggy Bauer

Brandon D. Cole/ENP Images

Page 146 **Florida manatee**

Trichechus manatus latirostris

Size: Up to 15 ft. length; 3,000 lb.

Breeding: Female (cow) gives birth once every three years after one-year gestation. Young nurses from teats under mother's flippers.

Traits: Herbivorous, eating more than 60 varieties of plants and grasses. Highly susceptible to cold. Moves freely between salt and fresh water.

Related Species: West Indian manatee.

Endangered: Yes.

Distribution: Florida peninsula primarily.

Conservation Efforts: CITES listing, protected under Florida Manatee Sanctuary Act, by boat speed laws and by no-boat zoning.

Page 140 **Thornbug**

Umbonia crassicornis

Size: 0.25 in.

Breeding: Eggs are inserted into slits in plant stems and overwinter there.

Traits: Treehopper whose body shape and coloration perfectly camouflage it as a thorn on woody plants. Young send vibrational signals to mother when threatened. The warning travels in a signaling wave through the colony.

Related Species: Spittlebug and other leafhoppers.

Endangered: No.

Distribution: California and Mexico.

Conservation Efforts: Habitat preservation.

Brian Kenney

Doug Perrine/Innerspace Visions

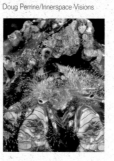

Page 147 **Hairy hermit crab**

Pagurus arcuatus

Size: 4–5 in. length.

Breeding: Eggs are held in the female's abdominal appendages until they hatch. Young seek out their own shells immediately upon hatching.

Traits: Scavenger. Uses snail shell or even the tubes of plant stems for shelter and protection. Periodically moves into larger shell as it grows.

Related Species: Approximately 4,500 species of crab.

Endangered: No.

Distribution: European and North American coastal waters and Galápagos Islands.

Conservation Efforts: Marine wildlife conservation acts, fishing restrictions.

Page 141 **Leaf-mimic katydid**

Typophyllum mortuifolium

Size: 1.75–2.2 in.

Breeding: Flat eggs inserted into bark, where they overwinter. Spring hatching.

Traits: Known for loud call of the male during courtship. Remains motionless in daytime.

Related Species: Grasshopper and cricket.

Endangered: No.

Distribution: Central and South American rain forest.

Conservation Efforts: Habitat preservation.

Kevin Schafer

Erwin and Peggy Bauer

Page 148 **Barn owl**

Tyto alba

Size: 14–20 in.; 43–47 in. wingspan.

Breeding: Mated pairs remain together many years. Four to seven eggs are laid in April, but a second brood may be laid later the same year if food is plentiful.

Traits: Nocturnal and solitary. Exceptional hearing. Virtually silent hunter of rats, mice, and insects. Returns to same nesting spot year after year. One of the most widespread species of birds on earth.

Related Species: Screech owl.

Endangered: No.

Distribution: Worldwide.

Conservation Efforts: Wildlife protection and conservation acts.

Pages 142–143 **Dead-leaf mantid**

Deroplatys sp.

Size: 3 in.

Breeding: Egg sac attached to weed stem and branch.

Traits: Highly predacious. Feeds on various insects. Ambushes prey with front legs raised.

Related Species: 1,800 mantid species.

Endangered: No.

Distribution: Indo-Malaysia.

Conservation Efforts: Habitat preservation, wildlife import and export controls.

Robert and Linda Mitchell

Erwin and Peggy Bauer

Page 149 **Argentine horned frog**

Ceratophrys ornata

Size: 4–5 in.

Breeding: Female spawns in shoals and male releases his sperm simultaneously. Eggs guarded by parents.

Traits: Cannibalistic. Large appetite. Resists drought by forming a cocoon around its body of sloughed layers of skin to seal in moisture. When drought ends, it eats the cocoon.

Related Species: Myobatrachidae family.

Endangered: No.

Distribution: Argentina, Uruguay, and Brazil.

Conservation Efforts: Habitat preservation, wildlife import and export controls.

Page 150 **Silky pygmy anteater**

Cyclopes didactylus

Size: 5–9 in. length, with 6–9 in. tail.

Breeding: Single young born after gestation of 120–150 days. Cared for and fed regurgitated insects by both parents.

Traits: Nocturnal, tiny, toothless mammal. Smallest of the anteaters. Feeds in treetops on insects only. Rarely descends to the ground.

Related Species: Sloth and armadillo.

Endangered: No.

Distribution: Mexico to northern Argentina.

Conservation Efforts: Habitat preservation.

Kevin Schafer

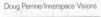

Doug Perrine/Innerspace Visions

Pages 158–159 **Spine-cheek anemonefish**

Premnas biaculeatus

Size: 2–6.5 in. Female is larger than male.

Breeding: All hatch as male, and some turn into female as they mature. Eggs are laid beneath the oral disc overhang of the anemone and are tended by the male.

Traits: Female is dominant, with a dominant male beneath her and all the other subadults beneath him in the hierarchy. Never found in nature apart from anemones.

Related Species: 28 species of anemonefish.

Endangered: No.

Distribution: Indo-Malayan Archipelago to northern Queensland.

Conservation Efforts: Marine wildlife conservation acts, wildlife import and export controls.

Page 151 **Red fox**

Vulpus vulpus

Size: 12–30 lb.

Breeding: Four to nine pups born eight weeks after mating. Mated pair remains together until young are raised.

Traits: Largest of North American foxes. Feeds on rodents and ground-nesting birds. Often nests in deserted marmot or fox dens. Young are often prey to golden eagles, coyote, and bobcats.

Related Species: Gray fox.

Endangered: No.

Distribution: Europe, Asia, Australia, and North America.

Conservation Efforts: Habitat preservation, regulated hunting.

Daniel J. Cox

Carol Polich

Page 161 **Meerkat**

Suricata suricata

Size: 20 in.; 2 lb.

Breeding: Two to four young born after gestation of 75 days. Breeds year-round.

Traits: Highly sociable. Average colony size is 24. Feeds largely on insects. Sentry, hunter, baby-sitter, teacher are some of the colony duties.

Related Species: Selous' mongoose.

Endangered: No.

Distribution: Southern Africa.

Conservation Efforts: Habitat preservation.

Pages 152–153 **Mule deer**

Odocoileus hemionus

Size: 264 lb. average.

Breeding: Breed in late November or early December. One to two young born after gestation of 204 days.

Traits: Remains on home range. Feeds on fruits, nuts, and leaves. Prey of bobcats, pumas, coyotes, golden eagles, and bears. Female remains with related females in clan. Male remains solitary or joins group of unrelated males.

Related Species: White-tailed deer.

Endangered: Yes, one subspecies.

Distribution: North America.

Conservation Efforts: CITES listing, wildlife reserves in native habitat.

Erwin and Peggy Bauer

Gary Vestal

Page 163 **Monarch butterfly**

Danaus plexippus

Size: 1 in.; 3 in. wingspan.

Breeding: Eggs hatch in three to four days. Caterpillars develop in three to four weeks.

Traits: Larvae feed on milkweed. Sometimes migrates 3,000 miles in North America. Winter roosting sites are in California and Mexico.

Related Species: African monarch butterfly.

Endangered: No.

Distribution: North and South America, Australia, Azores, New Zealand, and Indonesia.

Conservation Efforts: Habitat preservation.

Pages 154–155 **Nudibranch**

Hermissenda crasicornis

Size: 3–6 in.

Breeding: True hermaphrodite. Each carries both eggs and sperm and cross-fertilizes with others.

Traits: Also known as a sea slug, it is a shell-less snail. Beautiful coloring serves both as camouflage and warning to predators, as it is poisonous. Young has residual shell, which is shed in adulthood.

Related Species: Snails.

Endangered: No.

Distribution: Alaska to Baja California, Mexico.

Conservation Efforts: Marine wildlife conservation acts.

Richard Herrmann

Kevin Schafer

Page 164 **Leafcutter ant**

Atta cephalotes

Size: 0.4–0.5 in.

Breeding: Queen bites or rubs wings off after mating. Worker cares for immature stages until adulthood.

Traits: Lives in large underground colonies of up to one million, which can strip 20 percent of the leaves within half a mile of nest. Leaves are carried overhead to the colony but are not eaten. Instead they are used as mulch to raise a fungus garden attended by workers. The fungus is their only food.

Related Species: 8,000 species within Formicidae family.

Endangered: No.

Distribution: Neotropical areas of North, Central, and South America.

Conservation Efforts: Habitat preservation.

Pages 156–157 **Leopard**

Panthera pardus

Size: 23–28 in. height; 60–140 lb.

Breeding: Litters of one to three produced in two-year intervals. Gestation of 90–100 days.

Traits: Solitary. Extremely territorial. Prey is killed silently and taken up into a tree to be eaten.

Related Species: South American jaguar.

Endangered: Threatened.

Distribution: Pan-Africa and Asia.

Conservation Efforts: Regulated hunting, wildlife import and export controls.

Kevin Schafer

Art Wolfe

Page 166 **Indiana bat**

Myotis sodalis

Size: 0.3 oz.

Breeding: Pregnant female nests in maternity roosts. Single young per female is born in June or July. Mating just precedes hibernation, with sperm stored by the female all winter.

Traits: Extremely loyal to their chosen hibernation site, and location information is passed to succeeding generations.

Related Species: 900 species of flying bats.

Endangered: Yes.

Distribution: Eastern United States, particularly Indiana, Missouri, and Kentucky.

Conservation Efforts: CITES listing, Indiana Bat/Gray Bat Recovery Team assembled in the 1970s.

Page 167 **Greater and lesser flamingo**

Phoenicopterus ruber (greater)

Phoeniconaias minor (lesser)

Size: 35–59 in. (greater); 39 in. (lesser).

Breeding: One or two eggs incubated for one month by both parents.

Traits: Feeds on mollusks and crustaceans strained through the bill.

Related Species: Four species of tall wading birds.

Endangered: No.

Distribution: Greater: American Atlantic and Gulf coasts, Africa, Europe, and Asia. Lesser: Africa, Madagascar, and India.

Conservation Efforts: Wildlife protection and conservation acts.

Tim Fitzharris

Kevin Schafer

Page 175 **Ladybird beetle**

Hippodamia convergens

Size: 0.3–0.4 in. length.

Breeding: Larvae pass though four growth stages in four weeks and then pupate in the final stage.

Traits: Feeds on insects and insect eggs. Used by gardeners to control aphids. Dormant in winter. Called ladybug in the United States.

Related Species: 5,000 beetles of the same family.

Endangered: No.

Distribution: Western North America.

Conservation Efforts: Limitations on field clearing and burning.

Pages 168–169 **King penguin**

Aptenodytes patagonicus

Size: 37 in.; 20–33 lb.

Breeding: Male incubates eggs (62–66 days) while female leaves to feed. Male fasts throughout courtship, mating period, and incubation.

Traits: The most social of all birds. Usually forages in water over shelf and slope areas.

Related Species: 17 species of penguins.

Endangered: No.

Distribution: Sub-Antarctic islands and peninsulas.

Conservation Efforts: Marine wildlife conservation acts.

Kevin Schafer

Erwin and Peggy Bauer

Pages 176–177 **Musk-ox**

Ovibus moschatus

Size: 4–5 ft.; 400–800 lb.

Breeding: Late-summer breeding. Single young (22–31 lb.) born in spring to female older than two years.

Traits: Gregarious. Herds of up to 75 animals. Bull violently battles in mating season, charging others at full speed from 150 feet. Sound of impact can be heard a mile away. A battle may have up to 20 charges.

Related Species: Sheep and goats.

Endangered: No.

Distribution: Northern Canada and Alaska.

Conservation Efforts: Regulated hunting.

Pages 170–171 **Plain's zebra**

Equus burchelli

Size: 47–55 in. height; 400–500 lb.

Breeding: Single 70- to 80-pound foal born after one-year gestation. Foal gains 1 pound per day for first two months of life.

Traits: Small family groups may form mixed, migratory herds with antelopes and wildebeests. Spends 60–80 percent of its time feeding on fruits, grasses, roots, and bark.

Related Species: Grevy's zebra and mountain zebra.

Endangered: No.

Distribution: Eastern and southern Africa.

Conservation Efforts: Captive breeding programs, wildlife reserves in native habitiat.

Kevin Schafer

Kevin Schafer

Pages 178–179 **Sea nettle jellyfish**

Chrysaora fuscecens

Size: 10 in. width; 5 in. length.

Breeding: Reproduces asexually as well as sexually. Male fertilizes female, who releases larvae. Larvae grow into polyps, which can clone themselves.

Traits: No brain or heart, and body is 97 percent water. Propelled by pulsating motion. Tentacles sting and immobilize prey. Feeds on plankton. Very long tentacles.

Related Species: Moon jellies, lion's mane, elegant jellies.

Endangered: No.

Distribution: Pacific Ocean.

Conservation Efforts: Marine wildlife conservation acts.

Pages 172–173 **Tundra swan**

Cygnus columbianus

Size: 13 lb.

Breeding: Three to six eggs laid in early spring and guarded by pair. Hatch in late June.

Traits: Feeds on shellfish and aquatic vegetation. Forms monogamous pair. Migrates in autumn. Both fresh and saltwater habitats. Also called "whistling swan" for high note called by leader of flock in flight.

Related Species: Ducks and geese.

Endangered: Threatened.

Distribution: North America.

Conservation Efforts: Federally protected refuges along Carolina coasts.

Tom and Pat Leeson

Kevin Schafer

Page 180 **African lion**

Panthera leo

Size: 6–8 ft. plus 23–35 in. tail; 3 ft. height; 270–500 lb.

Breeding: One to three cubs born after gestation of 100–120 days.

Traits: Carnivorous. Prides are led by dominant male. Strongly territorial, nocturnal. Feeds primarily on large ungulates.

Related Species: Asiatic lion.

Endangered: Vulnerable.

Distribution: Sub-Saharan Africa,and India.

Conservation Efforts: Wildlife reserves in native habitat, captive breeding programs.

Page 174 **Sergeant major**

Abudefduf sexfasciatus

Size: 6–9 in.

Breeding: Eggs laid on rock or in crevice on cleared surface. Male guards eggs until hatching.

Traits: Inhabits coral or rocky reefs. Feeds on plankton and algae. Nonmigratory. Lives at depths of 3–49 feet. Highly territorial.

Related Species: 300 species of damselfish.

Endangered: No.

Distribution: All tropical seas.

Conservation Efforts: Marine wildlife conservation acts, wildlife import and export controls.

Jeremy Stafford-Deitsch/ENP Images

Jeremy Stafford-Deitsch/ENP Images

Page 181 **Moray eel**

Gymnothorax kidako

Size: 5–11 ft.

Breeding: July–September. Eggs float on sea surface until hatching.

Traits: Nocturnal predator inhabiting shallow water and rocky areas of tropical and subtropical seas. Teeth seize and hold prey; jaws lock. Bite can chip human bones. Thick scaleless skin. Flesh is toxic. Dead fish, blood, or bait will attract it.

Related Species: 80 species of eels.

Endangered: No.

Distribution: Indo-Pacific seas.

Conservation Efforts: Marine wildlife conservation acts.

Pages 182–183 **Emperor penguin**

Aptenodytes forsteri

Size: 4 ft.; 45–90 lb.

Breeding: June–August annual breeding period. Male incubates single egg, almost entirely without the female's help, on top of his feet under a loose fold of skin. Does not nest.

Traits: Largest of all penguins. Highly sociable and feeds at sea. Forms large colonies of 500 to 20,000 pairs.

Related Species: King penguin is closest of the 17 other species of penguins.

Endangered: No.

Distribution: Antarctica.

Conservation Efforts: Marine wildlife conservation acts.

Kevin Schafer

Tony Heald/the BBC/ENP Images

Pages 192–193 **African cheetah**

Acinonyx jubatus

Size: 55 in. length; 86–140 lb.

Breeding: Two to four kittens born after a gestation of about 95 days. Poor survival rate among kittens, which often fall prey to lions or hyenas.

Traits: The fastest land animal in the world. Adult is able to reach 60 mph. Female hunts alone by day, male in family groups.

Related Species: Northern Iran cheetah.

Endangered: Yes. Asian cheetah extinct in India.

Distribution: Sub-Saharan Africa and northern Iran.

Conservation Efforts: CITES listing, habitat preservation, wildlife reserves in native habitat.

Pages 184–185 **Walrus**

Odobenus rosmarus

Size: 7.5–10 ft. length; up to 1,700 lb.

Breeding: Mates in the water usually between December and March. Single calf is the norm with gestation of 15–16 months.

Traits: Male and female join separate herds, which congregate by the hundreds.

Related Species: Two walrus subspecies.

Endangered: No.

Distribution: Pacific walrus: Bering, Chukchi, and Laptev Seas. Atlantic walrus: coastal areas of northeastern Canada and Greenland.

Conservation Efforts: Marine wildlife conservation acts.

Kevin Schafer

Art Wolfe

Pages 194–195 **Wildebeest**

Connochaetes taurinus albojubatus

Size: 46–58 in. shoulder height; 300–600 lb.

Breeding: A single calf is born after eight to nine months, with virtually all calves of herd born within days of each other.

Traits: Fast-moving, nomadic antelope that grazes on open plains. Large herds remain near water sources. Migrating herds can contain a million animals.

Related Species: The white-bearded gnu is a subspecies of the blue wildebeest.

Endangered: No.

Distribution: Kenya, Tanzania, and into northeastern South Africa.

Conservation Efforts: Wildlife reserves in native habitat. Protection in Serengeti region have increased numbers dramatically.

Pages 186–187 **Schooling bannerfish**

Heniochus diphrentes

Size: Up to 9.8 in.

Breeding: Egg scatterer.

Traits: Travels in large schools. Diurnal, feeds on zooplankton. Enters a sleepy state at night, at which time it may change color.

Related Species: Butterfly fish.

Endangered: No.

Distribution: East Africa to Hawaiian islands.

Conservation Efforts: Marine wildlife conservation acts, wildlife import and export controls.

Doug Perrine/Innerspace Visions

Jeff Foott

Pages 196–197 **Sockeye salmon**

Oncorhynchus nerka

Size: 4–7 lb.; up to 33 in.

Breeding: Female and male spawn simultaneously into a gravel pit dug by the female in the same streambed where she and the male were born.

Traits: May migrate 1,000 miles or more to spawn, swimming against rapids and leaping up falls along the way. Color changes from silver to bright red as it travels upstream to spawn.

Related Species: Six species of Pacific salmon.

Endangered: No.

Distribution: Northern Bering Sea to Japan and North American Pacific.

Conservation Efforts: Commercial fishing restrictions.

Pages 188–189 **Bighorn sheep**

Ovis canadensis

Size: 50 in. height; up to 300 lb.

Breeding: Lambs born late February–May after a gestation of six months.

Traits: Both sexes have horns. Male uses its horns to fight for a harem at breeding time. Male and female with young form different herds. Migrated from Siberia over 10,000 years ago.

Related Species: Two species of North American sheep in Alaska and Canada.

Endangered: Vulnerable.

Distribution: Western United States and Canada.

Conservation Efforts: Regulated hunting.

Jeff Venuga

Erwin and Peggy Bauer

Page 199 **Western lowland gorilla**

Gorilla gorilla gorilla

Size: 4.6–5.6 ft. height; 198–397 lb.

Breeding: Year-round breeding. Female conceives for first time at 8 years. Male successfully breeds beginning at 11 years. Gestation of 258 days.

Traits: Nests and feeds in all forest types. Not strongly territorial. Groups of 2–30 inhabit home range of 2.2–2.7 miles, moving within it based on availability of seasonal fruits.

Related Species: Eastern lowland gorilla; 11 primate families.

Endangered: Yes.

Distribution: Cameroon, Central African Republic, Gabon, Congo, and Equatorial Guinea.

Conservation Efforts: CITES listing, captive breeding programs.

Pages 190–191 **Eastern white pelican**

Pelecanus onocrotalus

Size: 50–72 in.; 10–25 lb.

Breeding: All pairs within a colony are on the same reproductive cycle. One to four eggs hatch after incubation of one month.

Traits: Young feeds on food regurgitated by its parents. Fishes cooperatively. Throat pouch used as fishing net.

Related Species: Seven species of water birds with elastic throat pouches.

Endangered: No.

Distribution: Africa, southeast Europe, southern Asia, East Indies, and Australia.

Conservation Efforts: Habitat preservation, pesticide bans.

Erwin and Peggy Bauer

Jeff Foott

Page 200 **Sockeye salmon**

Oncorhynchus nerka

Size: 4–7 lb.; up to 33 in.

Breeding: Female and male spawn simultaneously into a gravel pit dug by the female. The eggs are then covered up and incubation takes 60–100 days, depending on water temperature.

Traits: One to two years after hatching, young migrate to the sea where they will spend two years before returning to the home stream.

Related Species: Six species of Pacific salmon.

Endangered: No.

Distribution: Northern Bering Sea to Japan and North American Pacific.

Conservation Efforts: Commercial fishing restrictions.

Page 201 **Sockeye salmon**
Oncorhynchus nerka
Size: 4–7 lb.; up to 33 in.
Breeding: Once it enters the stream, the salmon stops eating and has a single objective—to reach the spawn site and mate.
Traits: It is thought the salmon remembers the way to its home stream from its outward trip to the sea two years earlier.
Related Species: Six species of Pacific salmon.
Endangered: No.
Distribution: Northern Bering Sea to Japan and North American Pacific.
Conservation Efforts: Commercial fishing restrictions.

Kevin Schafer

Page 203 **Green sea turtle**
Chelonia mydas
Size: Up to 5 ft.; 400 lb.
Breeding: 75–200 eggs laid at night after gestation of 7–10 weeks. Eggs hatch in two to three months.
Traits: Young feeds on crustaceans and fish, adult feeds only on plants. Solitary. Prefers warm shallow waters.
Related Species: Seven species of sea turtle.
Endangered: Yes.
Distribution: Warm oceans and Mediterranean Sea.
Conservation Efforts: Marine wildlife preservation acts.

Kevin Schafer

Page 204 **African lion**
Panthera leo
Size: 6–8 ft. plus 23–35 in. tail; 3 ft. height; 270–500 lb.
Breeding: One to three cubs born after gestation of 100-120 days.
Traits: Carnivorous. Prides led by dominant male. Strongly territorial, nocturnal. Feeds primarily on large ungulates.
Related Species: Asiatic lion.
Endangered: Vulnerable.
Distribution: Sub-Saharan Africa and India.
Conservation Efforts: Wildlife reserves in native habitat, captive breeding programs.

Tom and Pat Leeson

Carol Polich

Pages 206–207 **Coyote**
Canis latrans
Size: 40–46 in. length; 19–30 lb. average.
Breeding: One to six young on average born early spring after gestation of 60–63 days. Male brings food to mate while awaiting the pups' birth. Pairs mate for life.
Traits: Hunts individually or in pairs. Nocturnal. Uses same den year after year. Acute hearing and sense of smell. Good swimmer.
Related Species: Domestic dog, wolf.
Endangered: No.
Distribution: North and Central America.
Conservation Efforts: Habitat preservation, regulated hunting.

Erwin and Peggy Bauer

Pages 208–209 **African elephant**
Loxodonta africana
Size: 10 ft. shoulder height; 3–6 tons.
Breeding: No particular breeding time. Single calf born after gestation of 22 months.
Traits: Herbivorous. Female lives in matriarchal herd. Young male lives in bachelor herd. Adult male is solitary. Very social with strong family ties.
Related Species: Asian elephant.
Endangered: Yes.
Distribution: Sub-Saharan Africa.
Conservation Efforts: CITES listing, wildlife reserves in native habitat, hunting bans on ivory.

Tim Davis and Renee Lynn

Page 224 **Chimpanzee**
Pan troglodytes
Size: 54–66 in.; 70–175 lb.
Breeding: One to two young born after gestation of 230–261 days. Female mates again when young are about three years old.
Traits: Highly sociable in small troops with a dominant male. Numerous and distinct facial expressions convey emotions. Uses sticks and leaves as tools. Intensively feeds early in the morning and late in the afternoon on fruit, insects, and, rarely, meat.
Related Species: Pygmy chimpanzees of Zaire.
Endangered: Yes.
Distribution: Central Africa.
Conservation Efforts: CITES listing, trapping for medical experimentation decreasing due to public pressure.

Technical Consultants

Erwin and Peggy Bauer
Wildlife photographers, naturalists, and authors. Sequim, Washington

Donal Boyer
Associate Curator of Reptiles, Zoological Society of San Diego, San Diego, California

Tim Cooke
Aquarist, Monterey Bay Aquarium, Monterey, California

David Faulkner
Entomologist, San Diego Natural History Museum, San Diego, California

Ed Lewins
Associate Curator of Birds, Zoological Society of San Diego, San Diego, California

Steve Manning
Naturalist/Environmental Affairs Officer, The Nature Company, Berkeley, California

Fernando Nosratpour
Senior Aquarist, Birch Aquarium at Scripps Scripps Institution of Oceanography, La Jolla, California

Carol Polich
Naturalist and photographer, Bozeman, Montana

Mary Sekulovich
Associate Editor, Zoonooz, and Editor, CRES Report, The Zoological Society of San Diego, San Diego, California

Index